TOEFL (with an

Part II
Intermediate

1300 multiple-choice items

Daniel B. Smith

Copyright © 2022

All rights reserved. No part of this publication may be reproduced, distributed or transmitted in any form or by any means, including photocopying, recording, or other electronic or mechanical methods, without the prior written permission of the author, excepting the case of brief quotations embodied in critical reviews and certain other noncommercial uses permitted by copyright law.

TOEFL GRAMMAR
with answer key

Part II
Intermediate

-1300 multiple-choice items-

Table of contents

Introduction 4
Set I 5
Set II 19
Set III 33
Set IV 48
Set V 63
Set VI 78
Set VII 93
Set VIII 108
Set IX 123
Set X 138
Set XI 153
Set XII 168
Set XIII 183
Answers 198
Conclusion 201

Introduction

The main purpose of these book series is to provide you an impressive and invaluable collection of TOEFL Grammar multiple-choice exercises with answers.

This book comprises different items and will take you on a beautiful journey towards improving your English for TOEFL exam.

There are three levels of difficulty in my "TOEFL Grammar with Answer Key" series: Beginner, Intermediate and Advanced. Choose the best that suits you and enhance your English knowledge.

This book deals with Intermediate English level and is the second book of the series.

Please keep an eye on further releases.
Good luck!

Set I

1. Choose the right answer: "You can join the club when you ... a bit older.".
    a) will have got
    b) get
    c) are getting

2. Choose the right answer: "If you ... your money to mine, we shall have enough to buy that car.".
    a) add
    b) combine
    c) join

3. Choose the right answer: "I'll phone as soon as I ... to Paris.".
    a) reach
    b) make
    c) get

4. Choose the right answer: "We decided ... at home this afternoon.".
    a) stay
    b) to stay
    c) staying

5. Choose the right answer: "He kept ... the same thing again and again.".
    a) repeat to
    b) repeat
    c) repeating

6. Choose the right answer: "They ... our party about eleven.".
    a) left
    b) leave
    c) leaving

7. Choose the right answer: "Paul ... with us for about nine days by now.".
    a) lived
    b) has lived
    c) had lived

8. Choose the right answer: "Last year I ... all of my books in this office.".
    a) keep

b) have kept
   c) kept

9. Choose the right answer: "I'm afraid I ... my gloves when I was walking home.".
   a) lost
   b) will loose
   c) have lost

10. Choose the right answer: "She prefers cycling ... driving.".
    a) than
    b) to
    c) for

11. Choose the right answer: "She used to visit you quite often, ...?".
    a) didn't she
    b) wouldn't she
    c) hadn't she

12. Choose the right answer: "After the way they treated you, if I ... in your place, I wouldn't return the call.".
    a) be
    b) was
    c) were

13. Choose the right answer: "I think that you had better ... earlier so that you can get to class on time.".
    a) to get up
    b) start getting up
    c) started getting up

14. Choose the right answer: "I have finished typing all ... the last page.".
    a) but
    b) until
    c) for

15. Choose the right answer: "There is no reason to ... the man simply because you do not agree with him.".
    a) enhance
    b) defame
    c) animate

16. Choose the right answer: "She's a sharp cookie. There's no way anybody can pull the wool over her …".
	a) tissue
	b) grass
	c) eyes

17. Choose the right answer: "If that firm wants to attract workers, it must … the pay.".
	a) raise
	b) lower
	c) rise

18. Choose the right answer: "The lung transplant operation was … complicated.".
	a) broadly
	b) immediately
	c) extremely

19. Choose the right answer: "Her boss is sometimes forgetful … the promises he has made.".
	a) of
	b) at
	c) to

20. Choose the right answer: "I am glad so many people have passed the test. In fact, they were … who haven't.".
	a) little
	b) few
	c) a little

21. Choose the right answer: "The funeral will be …, and only members of the dead man's family will attend.".
	a) private
	b) alone
	c) peculiar

22. Choose the right answer: "Do you really believe … ghosts?".
	a) for
	b) about
	c) in

23. Choose the right answer: "I enjoyed ... her again after all this time.".
   a) to see
   b) seeing
   c) to seeing

24. Choose the right answer: "I am sorry that I can't ... your invitation.".
   a) accept
   b) take
   c) have

25. Choose the right answer: "When he was a boy, he was always willing to join in a ... of football.".
   a) play
   b) group
   c) game

26. Choose the right answer: "The next ... of the committee will take place on Friday.".
   a) meeting
   b) collection
   c) group

27. Choose the right answer: "Who ... the boss tell him that?".
   a) does hear
   b) heard
   c) did hear

28. Choose the right answer: "His parents never allowed him ...".
   a) a smoking
   b) to smoke
   c) smoking

29. Choose the right answer: "I have absolutely no doubt ... the innocence of the accused.".
   a) about
   b) over
   c) on

30. Choose the right answer: "As she had distinctions in Chemistry and Biology, I hoped to ... one of these subjects at university.".
   a) abandon

b) take
c) specialize in

31. Choose the right answer: "The room was infested ... cockroaches.".
    a) to
    b) by
    c) with

32. Choose the right answer: "In my company only executives are eligible ... share option schemes.".
    a) for
    b) with
    c) of

33. Choose the right answer: "Bill is simply blind ... his own shortcomings.".
    a) with
    b) to
    c) at

34. Choose the right answer: "She was born ... two intelligent people.".
    a) to
    b) of
    c) with

35. Choose the right answer: "Dave took a taxi ... he wouldn't be late.".
    a) unless
    b) even so
    c) so that

36. Choose the right answer: "He went to a school which ... good manners and self-discipline.".
    a) grew
    b) cultivated
    c) planted

37. Choose the right answer: "She ... 20 pounds out of the bank every Friday.".
    a) draws
    b) pulls
    c) takes

38. Choose the right answer: "The lost of a front tooth has left an unsightly ... in her teeth.".

a) slot
   b) gap
   c) hole

39. Choose the right answer: "The terms refer to different animals and careful students ... the two.".
   a) ignore
   b) intermingle
   c) distinguish

40. Choose the right answer: "Although the terms toad and frog refer to different animals belonging to different genres, some students ... the two.".
   a) confuse
   b) respect
   c) observe

41. Choose the right answer: "His new ... fitted so badly across the shoulders that he took it back to the shop to complain.".
   a) shirt
   b) strap
   c) sheet

42. Choose the right answer: "I'll go on holiday ... I can.".
   a) as
   b) until
   c) as soon as

43. Choose the right answer: "Would you like ... that for you?".
   a) me doing
   b) me do
   c) me to do

44. Choose the right answer: "They ... our new transistor radio before.".
   a) have never seen
   b) never see
   c) didn't see

45. Choose the right answer: "She said she ... to me, but she didn't.".
   a) will write
   b) would write
   c) would have written

46. Choose the right answer: "If it ... so late I could have coffee.".
    a) weren't
    b) isn't
    c) not be

47. Choose the right answer: "I'd rather you ... anything about it for the time being.".
    a) do
    b) didn't do
    c) don't

48. Choose the right answer: "I wish that the weather ... not so warm.".
    a) be
    b) were
    c) is

49. Choose the right answer: "I walked away as calmly as I could ... they thought I was the thief.".
    a) or else
    b) owing to
    c) in case

50. Choose the right answer: "Although he has ..., his poor writing often clouds his thoughts.".
    a) good grammar
    b) excellent ideas
    c) good instructors

51. Choose the right answer: "She's gone already? I am only ... minutes late!".
    a) a few
    b) a little
    c) little

52. Choose the right answer: "When he was questioned by the police, the thief didn't ... the truth.".
    a) reply
    b) answer
    c) tell

53. Choose the right answer: "To get money for some purpose is to ...".
    a) donate it

b) raise it

c) increase it

54. Choose the right answer: "I ran quickly …. late.".
    a) in order to be not
    b) in order to not be
    c) in order not to be

55. Choose the right answer: "I bought … yesterday.".
    a) a pair of trousers
    b) a trouser
    c) a trousers

56. Choose the right answer: "What does he do for a living? He is …".
    a) bus driver
    b) a bus driver
    c) bus' driver

57. Choose the right answer: "… there in time, we must start now.".
    a) Being
    b) Be
    c) To be

58. Choose the right answer: "They have made a lot of progress … the country became independent.".
    a) before
    b) since
    c) for

59. Choose the right answer: "The Boeing is twice … that plane.".
    a) bigger than
    b) as big as
    c) as bigger as

60. Choose the right answer: "They are hanging up their clothes to make them …".
    a) dry
    b) being dry
    c) drying

61. Choose the right answer: "I go …. school in the morning.".
    a) at

b) for
c) to

62. Choose the right answer: "Would you like … to one of my friend about it?".
    a) talking
    b) to talk
    c) talk

63. Choose the right answer: "Mr. Smith … me a very nice letter a few days ago.".
    a) sends
    b) sent
    c) have sent

64. Choose the right answer: "She … a very amusing article in one of the newspapers yesterday.".
    a) found
    b) finds
    c) had found

65. Choose the right answer: "They are … their competition now.".
    a) start
    b) started
    c) starting

66. Choose the right answer: "She got … bronchitis and was taken to … hospital.".
    a) a/a
    b) -/-
    c) the/a

67. Choose the right answer: "It was raining … so we couldn't go out.".
    a) all day
    b) all the days
    c) every days

68. Choose the right answer: "…, please. I'll see if the manager is in.".
    a) Ring off
    b) Hang up
    c) Hold on

69. Choose the right answer: "Since your roommate is visiting her family this weekend, ... you like to have dinner with us tonight?".
   a) will
   b) wouldn't
   c) do

70. Choose the right answer: "The old man asked her to move because he ... in that chair.".
   a) was used to sitting
   b) used to sitting
   c) was used to sit

71. Choose the right answer: "Excuse me, but it is time to have your temperature ...".
   a) taking
   b) take
   c) taken

72. Choose the right answer: "The ticket agent said that the plane would be boarding at ...".
   a) the gave five
   b) the five gate
   c) gate five

73. Choose the right answer: "At a potluck dinner, everyone who comes must .... a dish.".
   a) bring
   b) take
   c) carry

74. Choose the right answer: "Just put your coat in ...".
   a) hall closet
   b) the hall closet
   c) the hall's closet

75. Choose the right answer: "On the ... to the town there is a beautiful wood.".
   a) direction
   b) way
   c) entrance

76. Choose the right answer: "But why did the police suspect you? It just doesn't make … to me.".
    a) reason
    b) sense
    c) truth

77. Choose the right answer: "If something is out of order, it is …".
    a) off-limits
    b) fashionable
    c) not in working condition

78. Choose the right answer: "The tenants were … not to disturb other tenants after 1 p.m.".
    a) requested
    b) informed
    c) appealed

79. Choose the right answer: "This house … five rooms.".
    a) is consisted
    b) consists of
    c) consists

80. Choose the right answer: "I don't know where he lives; I don't … know who he is.".
    a) moreover
    b) as well
    c) even

81. Choose the right answer: "Take the juice … the fridge.".
    a) into
    b) in
    c) out of

82. Choose the right answer: "You can eat … you like!".
    a) as much as
    b) so much
    c) as much that

83. Choose the right answer: "After the battle, the … soldiers were helped.".
    a) broken

b) wounded
c) damaged

84. Choose the right answer: "I apologize ... not writing sooner.".
    a) of
    b) for
    c) to

85. Choose the right answer: "I do ... I could speak German well.".
    a) wish
    b) like
    c) know

86. Choose the right answer: "Don't you think you ought ... much harder?".
    a) working
    b) work to
    c) to work

87. Choose the right answer: "Her parents made her ... very hard.".
    a) work
    b) to work
    c) be working

88. Choose the right answer: "They ... Spanish for about two years so far.".
    a) study
    b) have studied
    c) studied

89. Choose the right answer: "We ... it with Dave and Mary a month ago.".
    a) had discussed
    b) discussed
    c) have discussed

90. Choose the right answer: "We eat ... soup with ... spoon.".
    a) the/the
    b) a/a
    c) -/a

91. Choose the right answer: "Since they aren't answering their telephone, they ...".
    a) should have left
    b) can have left
    c) must have left

92. Choose the right answer: "If you want to find good information, look in ... of the Advanced Science Books.".
    a) volume two
    b) volume second
    c) the volume two

93. Choose the right answer: "Almost every citizen of a large city suffers ... of organized crime.".
    a) as a result of the debility
    b) from the depredations
    c) from the deletion

94. Choose the right answer: "Her feeling of ebullience was so contagious that all the other patients ...".
    a) began to weep
    b) became very anxious
    c) were soon smiling

95. Choose the right answer: "Our Constitution was based on the belief that the free interchange of ideas ... the preservation of a democratic society.".
    a) would sure help
    b) can devastate
    c) is essential to

96. Choose the right answer: "If you take a train of a bus, you must pay a ...".
    a) fare
    b) tip
    c) fee

97. Choose the right answer: "... we had driving in the country!".
    a) How wonderful day
    b) What a wonderful day
    c) What the wonderful day

98. Choose the right answer: "He went to a seaside resort because he was ... on water-skiing.".
    a) keen
    b) interested
    c) impassioned

99. Choose the right answer: "How … meat did you buy?".
> a) few
> b) much
> c) many

100. Choose the right answer: "The value of money is … and can be … by supply and demand.".
> a) predetermined/overruled
> b) lackluster/improved
> c) arbitrary/altered

Set II

101. Choose the right answer: "Put the butter ... the fridge.".
    a) into
    b) off
    c) out

102. Choose the right answer: "The hotel is next ... the bank.".
    a) from
    b) on
    c) to

103. Choose the right answer: "I must have dropped my wallet ... in the street.".
    a) off
    b) -
    c) out

104. Choose the right answer: "She grew very angry when she realized how she had been ... out of her money.".
    a) played
    b) robbed
    c) tricked

105. Choose the right answer: "We ... to take a walk now.".
    a) are going
    b) can
    c) will

106. Choose the right answer: "The visitors ... all the different ways of making brandy.".
    a) has shown
    b) were shown
    c) had shown

107. Choose the right answer: "We wish that you ... such a lot of work, because we know that you would have enjoyed the party.".
    a) didn't have
    b) hadn't have
    c) hadn't

108. Choose the right answer: "Would you mind …, please?".
    a) answering the telephone
    b) to answer the telephone
    c) to the telephone answering

109. Choose the right answer: "We were hurrying because we thought that the bell … .".
    a) have already ringing
    b) have already rung
    c) had already rung

110. Choose the right answer: "She has taken her medicine, …?".
    a) didn't she
    b) hasn't she
    c) doesn't she

111. Choose the right answer: "I'll have a cup of tea and …".
    a) two toasts
    b) two pieces of toast
    c) two pieces of toasts

112. Choose the right answer: "If you don't have an answer from the University, why … call the admissions office?".
    a) not
    b) not to
    c) don't

113. Choose the right answer: "The television program … but also entertaining.".
    a) is not only amusing
    b) is not simply enjoyable
    c) is not only informative

114. Choose the right answer: "Paris lies … the river Seine.".
    a) on
    b) over
    c) at

115. Choose the right answer: "The rise in house prices … him to sell his house for a large profit.".
    a) facilitated

b) enabled

c) achieved

116. Choose the right answer: "They arrived at the destination …".

a) save

b) safely

c) savely

117. Choose the right answer: "The public debates were often …, finally deteriorating into contests.".

a) informative

b) inspiring

c) bitter

118. Choose the right answer: "Despite the fact that they had clinched the divisional title, the team continued to play every game as though it were …".

a) vital

b) irrational

c) hopeless

119. Choose the right answer: "If he … lucky, he can get the job.".

a) had been

b) would be

c) is

120. Choose the right answer: "If I … the flu I would have gone with you.".

a) didn't have

b) hadn't

c) hadn't had

121. Choose the right answer: "I come home … school in the afternoon.".

a) at

b) from

b) in

122. Choose the right answer: "When my aunt lost her cat last summer, it turned … a week later at a house in the next village.".

a) up

b) in

c) out

123. Choose the right answer: "My old cat died last year and I still ... her.".
   a) fail
   b) lose
   c) miss

124. Choose the right answer: "At the first ... of twelve everybody stopped for lunch.".
   a) minute
   b) stroke
   c) strike

125. Choose the right answer: "We ... her a happy birthday.".
   a) wished
   b) said
   c) told

126. Choose the right answer: "Yesterday he ... me a very interesting story.".
   a) tells
   b) told
   c) has told

127. Choose the right answer: "... your math course yet?".
   a) do you start
   b) did you started
   c) have you started

128. Choose the right answer: "I ... from Steven for more than a week.".
   a) don't hear
   b) doesn't hear
   c) haven't heard

129. Choose the right answer: "My friend ... when the lesson started.".
   a) wasn't arriving
   b) hadn't arrived
   c) hasn't arrived

130. Choose the right answer: "Would you please ... write on the test books?".
   a) not
   b) to not
   c) don't

131. Choose the right answer: "... your rather sit by the window?".
    a) Don't
    b) Wouldn't
    c) Will

132. Choose the right answer: "She is a really annoying person. She's always getting ... my nose.".
    a) in
    b) on
    c) up

133. Choose the right answer: "I've never heard such a load of cock and ... my life.".
    a) bull
    b) pack
    c) fishy

134. Choose the right answer: "This country, for the present, is deeply mired ... and the future looks uncertain.".
    a) in a such mess
    b) in economic troubles
    c) in a lot of problems

135. Choose the right answer: "When water is heated, it will change into ...".
    a) bubble
    b) foam
    c) vapour

136. Choose the right answer: "Each of them ... to bring ... own book to the next class.".
    a) is/his
    b) is/theirs
    c) are/his

137. Choose the right answer: "This area is ... a nice place that they want to live there.".
    a) so
    b) such
    c) so that

138. Choose the right answer: "A sword will only draw blood if it actually … the skin.".
    a) sticks
    b) pricks
    c) pierces

139. Choose the right answer: "Before joining a course of study you must fill in a long … form.".
    a) enrolment
    b) inscription
    c) inception

140. Choose the right answer: "You can see a second-hand car only if it is in reasonably good …".
    a) state
    b) condition
    c) standing

141. Choose the right answer: "Mark hoped the appointment would enable him to gain greater … in publishing.".
    a) work
    b) experience
    c) jobs

142. Choose the right answer: "Your room is a mess! … it up at once!".
    a) Do
    b) Make
    c) Tidy

143. Choose the right answer: "Large waves were … on the seashore.".
    a) breaking
    b) coming
    c) running

144. Choose the right answer: "Their house is … near the church.".
    a) whereabouts
    b) anywhere
    c) somewhere

145. Choose the right answer: "There was hardly … money left in the bank account.".
    a) more

b) any
c) no

146. Choose the right answer: "They were making enough noise at the party to wake the …".
    a) people
    b) dead
    c) company

147. Choose the right answer: "Can you … me 20 euros until next week?".
    a) lend
    b) borrow
    c) rent

148. Choose the right answer: "As far as I know, she … back yet.".
    a) don't come
    b) isn't coming
    c) hasn't come

149. Choose the right answer: "I've decided to join … this club.".
    a) -
    b) to
    c) at

150. Choose the right answer: "Are you sure Ms. Smith … use the new equipment?".
    a) knows to
    b) knows how
    c) knows how to

151. Choose the right answer: "His government insisted that she … until she finished her degree.".
    a) should stay
    b) stayed
    c) shall stay

152. Choose the right answer: "Because they receive the same score on exams, there is often disagreement as to … is the better student, Steve or Mary.".
    a) whose
    b) who
    c) which

153. Choose the right answer: "She remembered the correct address only ... she had posted the letter.".
   a) since
   b) after
   c) following

154. Choose the right answer: "The managers agreed to ... the question of payment.".
   a) balance
   b) increase
   c) discuss

155. Choose the right answer: "When she left school, Sara decided to ... a priest instead of studying languages.".
   a) become
   b) study
   c) train for

156. Choose the right answer: "This is clearly not true – just a ... and bull story.".
   a) fishy
   b) teeth
   c) cock

157. Choose the right answer: "Your sister is very tall. What is her exact ...?".
   a) length
   b) height
   c) size

158. Choose the right answer: "Studying late at night is one of those things that ... me tried.".
   a) makes
   b) make
   c) making

159. Choose the right answer: "He is a man who won't ... his promise.".
   a) break
   b) destroy
   c) run

160. Choose the right answer: "… that he only started learning three years ago, his English is excellent.".
    a) Accounting
    b) Thinking
    c) Considering

161. Choose the right answer: "There is … that I may have to go into hospital next week.".
    a) a possibility
    b) bad luck
    c) an opportunity

162. Choose the right answer: "Call for me at any time that … you.".
    a) does
    b) suits
    c) likes

163. Choose the right answer: "She always wore a shirt with an open …".
    a) tie
    b) top
    c) collar

164. Choose the right answer: "I have learned all the irregular verbs …".
    a) by heart
    b) in the memory
    c) from memory

165. Choose the right answer: "The soldiers were put in prison because they … to obey orders.".
    a) denied
    b) refused
    c) rejected

166. Choose the right answer: "I don't believe she can … it properly.".
    a) to do
    b) doing
    c) do

167. Choose the right answer: "I … as ill as I do now for a long time.".
    a) haven't felt
    b) didn't feel
    c) wasn't feeling

168. Choose the right answer: "If he … lucky, he can get the job.".
a) had been
b) is
c) would be

169. Choose the right answer: "Does your new secretary … shorthand?".
a) know how take
b) know to take
c) know how to take

170. Choose the right answer: "We … to the parties at the student union every Saturday.".
a) used to go
b) use to go
c) are used to go

171. Choose the right answer: "Michael had hoped … his letter.".
a) her to answer
b) that she would answer
c) her answering

172. Choose the right answer: "They forgot about … them to join us for lunch.".
a) us to asking
b) we asking
c) our asking

173. Choose the right answer: "I really appreciate … to help me.".
a) your offering
b) that you offer
c) you to offer

174. Choose the right answer: "It's difficult to pay one's bills when prices keep …".
a) growing
b) rising
c) gaining

175. Choose the right answer: "We have no … in our files of your recent letter to the tax office.".
a) memory

b) list

c) account

176. Choose the right answer: "They said they had the European rights for the product but it was a lie. They were acting under false …".

a) pretences

b) egg

c) wool

177. Choose the right answer: "The time is up. This means that the period of time has …".

a) begun

b) seemed long

c) ended

178. Choose the right answer: "… we dislike him, he's efficient and we can't dismiss him.".

a) As much

b) However much

c) Much

179. Choose the right answer: "The examiners often … extremely difficult questions for the literature exam.".

a) set

b) write

c) create

180. Choose the right answer: "All we see is the … of the iceberg.".

a) top

b) summit

c) tip

181. Choose the right answer: "This young tree could not have been damaged by accident: I believe it was done …".

a) on purpose

b) in fact

c) by plan

182. Choose the right answer: "I'm afraid I've got … my doctor today.".

a) see

b) to see

c) seeing

183. Choose the right answer: "I'd ... the operation unless it is absolutely necessary.".
    a) not rather had
    b) rather not having
    c) rather not have

184. Choose the right answer: "The brakes need ...".
    a) adjusted
    b) adjusting
    c) to adjustment

185. Choose the right answer: "If it ... rain, we'll have the party outside.".
    a) doesn't
    b) didn't
    c) won't

186. Choose the right answer: "A few of ... are planning to drive to Spain during spring break.".
    a) us boys
    b) we boys
    c) boys

187. Choose the right answer: "Please go to ... to pick up your ID card.".
    a) the window three
    b) the third window
    c) window third

188. Choose the right answer: "It's a beautiful car, but it is not ... the price.".
    a) value
    b) worthy
    c) worth

189. Choose the right answer: "I don't think she'll ever ... the shock of her husband's death.".
    a) get over
    b) get by
    c) get through

190. Choose the right answer: "The child hurt himself badly when he fell ... the bedroom window.".
    a) down

b) out of

c) over

191. Choose the right answer: "He … me to buy my air ticket immediately or it would be too late.".

    a) convinced

    b) advised

    c) insisted

192. Choose the right answer: "Dave got out of bed and took a few … but couldn't go any farther.".

    a) stages

    b) actions

    c) steps

193. Choose the right answer: "His performance was …; the audience was delighted.".

    a) faultless

    b) worthless

    c) imperfect

194. Choose the right answer: "I'm sure I'll find a way of getting … their objections.".

    a) round

    b) with

    c) away from

195. Choose the right answer: "The High Street is so narrow that they have decided to … it.".

    a) increase

    b) widen

    c) extend

196. Choose the right answer: "A box in which a dead person is buried is a …".

    a) tomb

    b) ditch

    c) coffin

197. Choose the right answer: "Most of us like … to the sea in summer.".

    a) going

b) gone
c) to be going

198. Choose the right answer: "I ... the hot weather in Thailand.".
   a) use to
   b) am used to
   c) uses to

199. Choose the right answer: "It's ... a nice day ... we should do something.".
   a) either/or
   b) neither/nor
   c) such/that

200. Choose the right answer: "The company went bankrupt and their shares became ...".
   a) worthless
   b) priceless
   c) unworthy

Set III

201. Choose the right answer: "Could you ... me ten pounds until next payday?".
    a) let
    b) provide
    c) lend

202. Choose the right answer: "Many kinds of ... animals are disappearing or have already disappeared from the earth.".
    a) wild
    b) angry
    c) brave

203. Choose the right answer: "I ... away for the next weekend.".
    a) go
    b) am going to go
    c) had

204. Choose the right answer: "She told him that if he ... his promise, she ... speak to him again.".
    a) break/would never
    b) broke/will never
    c) broke/would never

205. Choose the right answer: "They claimed they ... the law.".
    a) were not breaking
    b) hadn't broken
    c) wouldn't breaking

206. Choose the right answer: "I wish that we ... with my brother when he flies to England next week.".
    a) had gone
    b) will go
    c) could go

207. Choose the right answer: "The man who was driving the truck would not admit that he had been at fault and ...".
    a) the other driver neither

b) neither would the other driver
c) neither the other driver

208. Choose the right answer: "John Kennedy was ... of the United States.".
a) president the thirty-five
b) the thirty-fifth president
c) the president thirty-fifth

209. Choose the right answer: "Even when his reputation was in eclipse, almost everyone ... that he had genius.".
a) was willing to admit
b) swore on a stack of Bibles
c) denying vehemently

210. Choose the right answer: "When he heard the terrible noise he asked me what was ... on.".
a) being
b) happening
c) going

211. Choose the right answer: "Do you ... my turning the television on now?".
a) want
b) mind
c) object

212. Choose the right answer: "You're really old-fashioned. It's time you got more ... it.".
a) at
b) on
c) with

213. Choose the right answer: "They fooled me totally. They pulled the ... over my eyes.".
a) wool
b) snake
c) egg

214. Choose the right answer: "Too many undergraduates think it's easy to ... a job once they leave university.".
  a) obtain
  b) attain
  c) collect

215. Choose the right answer: "Everything about her is borrowed, temporary, unstable ...".
  a) like her clothing
  b) as a soap bubble
  c) with no regret

216. Choose the right answer: "The trunk of a tree is called the ...".
  a) root
  b) branch
  c) stem

217. Choose the right answer: "I hope you don't mind ... to come and meet her.".
  a) being asked
  b) to be asked
  c) you were asked

218. Choose the right answer: "Look at these two pieces of material I have just bought. Which do you like ...?".
  a) most
  b) better
  c) more than

219. Choose the right answer: "What pretty ... earrings you are wearing!".
  a) minor
  b) little
  c) huge

220. Choose the right answer: "They claimed they ... the law.".
  a) were not breaking
  b) haven't broken
  c) hadn't broken

221. Choose the right answer: "Where do you ... going for your holidays this year.".
- a) expect
- b) pretend
- c) intend

222. Choose the right answer: "It isn't quite ... that he will be present at the meeting.".
- a) right
- b) exact
- c) certain

223. Choose the right answer: "I always ... to the university by bus because it is much faster.".
- a) go
- b) had gone
- c) have gone

224. Choose the right answer: "You are not half ... you think you are.".
- a) as clever like
- b) as clever as
- c) as clever than

225. Choose the right answer: "I wish I ... younger.".
- a) were
- b) would be
- c) had been

226. Choose the right answer: "You ... a three-month contract when you are offered a permanent position elsewhere. What will you do?".
- a) started
- b) had started
- c) have just started

227. Choose the right answer: "I'll see you in August when I ... back.".
- a) will come
- b) came
- c) come

228. Choose the right answer: "As soon as you ... that, I'd like you to go to bed.".
    a) will do
    b) have done
    c) did

229. Choose the right answer: "My husband lived at home before we were married, and so ...".
    a) did I
    b) had I
    c) I did

230. Choose the right answer: "Let's go out for a drink, ...?".
    a) will we
    b) don't we
    c) shall we

231. Choose the right answer: "You ... me, because I didn't say that.".
    a) must have misunderstood
    b) must misunderstand
    c) had to misunderstand

232. Choose the right answer: "Mother's Day is ... May.".
    a) at
    b) in
    c) for

233. Choose the right answer: "Could you lend me some money? I'm very ... of cash at the moment.".
    a) down
    b) short
    c) scarce

234. Choose the right answer: "They are always ... with each other about money.".
    a) shouting
    b) annoying
    c) arguing

235. Choose the right answer: "I am late because my alarm clock never ... this morning.".
- a) went off
- b) came on
- c) turned on

236. Choose the right answer: "From now on I am not liable ... my sister's debts.".
- a) to
- b) for
- c) with

237. Choose the right answer: "He ... the river yesterday.".
- a) across
- b) crossing
- c) crossed

238. Choose the right answer: "Finding the money is just one of the problems ... in buying a house.".
- a) involved
- b) united
- c) gathered

239. Choose the right answer: "I am very ... your society and I want more details about it.".
- a) involved with
- b) interested in
- c) absorbed from

240. Choose the right answer: "Scientists have found that certain elements long known to be ... in large quantities are ... to life in small amounts.".
- a) lethal/essential
- b) deadly/painful
- c) fatal/unbearable

241. Choose the right answer: "Sarah walked ... the room.".
- a) over
- b) at
- c) into

242. Choose the right answer: "We are very proud … our sister's success.".
    a) of
    b) for
    c) on

243. Choose the right answer: "… what he says, he wasn't even there when the incident happened.".
    a) Hearing
    b) According to
    c) Following

244. Choose the right answer: "He … this kind of music at all.".
    a) don't like
    b) likes
    c) doesn't like

245. Choose the right answer: "Who … this window? It's so cold here.".
    a) opening
    b) has opened
    c) is going to open

246. Choose the right answer: "She is … her sister.".
    a) very taller than
    b) much taller then
    c) much taller than

247. Choose the right answer: "A new motorway … here next year.".
    a) will be built
    b) will build
    c) will have build

248. Choose the right answer: "I … on the bank fishing when I … a hat floating down the river.".
    a) was sitting/saw
    b) sat/was seeing
    c) has sat/had seen

249. Choose the right answer: "I … the flowers yesterday morning.".
    a) have watered

b) watered

c) have been watering

250. Choose the right answer: "Brian was the only foreigner ... I saw there.".
    a) which
    b) what
    c) whom

251. Choose the right answer: "The assignment for Monday was to read ... in your textbooks.".
    a) the tenth chapter
    b) chapter tenth
    c) chapter the tenth

252. Choose the right answer: "My English is far from perfect but I know enough to get ...".
    a) with
    b) by
    c) over

253. Choose the right answer: "The police finally arrested the ... criminal.".
    a) famous
    b) renowned
    c) notorious

254. Choose the right answer: "The architect received honorable mention for ... design.".
    a) designing a
    b) his unique
    c) his nice

255. Choose the right answer: "There is ... doubt that her team will win the quiz.".
    a) little
    b) few
    c) a few

256. Choose the right answer: "The national ... is the national song of the country.".

a) music
b) anthem
c) melody

257. Choose the right answer: "We found the trip to Europe …".
   a) excited
   b) was exciting
   c) exciting

258. Choose the right answer: "These shoes are …".
   a) my wife's
   b) my wives
   c) of my wife

259. Choose the right answer: "It's often better to … safe in exams than to give an original answer.".
   a) act
   b) play
   c) make

260. Choose the right answer: "Unless we … our water resources, there may come a time when our supplies of clean water are completely exhausted.".
   a) predict
   b) use
   c) conserve

261. Choose the right answer: "I had … decided to take a coat when it started to rain.".
   a) still
   b) already
   c) never

262. Choose the right answer: "I'm sorry I … able to see you yesterday.".
   a) can't
   b) didn't
   c) wasn't

263. Choose the right answer: "I can't advise you what to do; you must use your own …".

a) judgement
b) opinion
c) justice

264. Choose the right answer: "I ... to any of these meetings since last December.".
a) has been
b) haven't been
c) had been

265. Choose the right answer: "... to professor Smith since last Friday?".
a) Have you talked
b) Did you talk
c) Had you talked

266. Choose the right answer: "There was ... I could say.".
a) any
b) nothing
c) anything

267. Choose the right answer: "Today's weather isn't as cold as it was yesterday, ...?".
a) was it
b) isn't it
c) is it

268. Choose the right answer: "The policeman told the driver to pull over and asked, ...?".
a) what's your hurry, sir
b) let me see you licence
c) you could have caused an accident

269. Choose the right answer: "The other driver failed to signal his ... to turn right.".
a) design
b) intention
c) purpose

270. Choose the right answer: "Ms. Smith decided to give up her job for the ... of her children.".

a) care
b) reason
c) sake

271. Choose the right answer: "Stop criticizing me all the time! You never stop getting … me.".
　　a) at
　　b) in
　　c) on

272. Choose the right answer: "She's not the sort of person to trust. She's a bad …".
　　a) talker
　　b) egg
　　c) snake

273. Choose the right answer: "Unfortunately, … built up during the race and most of the boats turned to and went home.".
　　a) a snarling wind
　　b) a favorable wind
　　c) a light breeze

274. Choose the right answer: "Sarah is two years … than me.".
　　a) elder
　　b) old
　　c) older

275. Choose the right answer: "… he leaves or I leave.".
　　a) Neither
　　b) Either
　　c) Only

276. Choose the right answer: "If the prisoners attempt to escape from prison …".
　　a) he will catch
　　b) they will catch
　　c) they will be caught

277. Choose the right answer: "No educational system is perfect. Each one has its …".

a) borders
b) fence
c) limitations

278. Choose the right answer: "He's not very sensible as far as money ... are concerned.".
a) aspects
b) things
c) points

279. Choose the right answer: "We all know ... he is at boxing.".
a) how well
b) how good
c) how best

280. Choose the right answer: "Our plane will arrive ... Paris at noon.".
a) to
b) in
c) at

281. Choose the right answer: "The bridge goes ... the river.".
a) for
b) over
c) at

282. Choose the right answer: "Tell me the reason ... you said that.".
a) why
b) which
c) for

283. Choose the right answer: "I shall be working late ... office this evening.".
a) at
b) in
c) at the

284. Choose the right answer: "Steve has ... his job and gone back to college.".
a) given up

b) let off

c) passed up

285. Choose the right answer: "I don't think he would mind ... there with me.".

a) go

b) to go

c) going

286. Choose the right answer: "This is the woman ... the renowned artist said posed as a model for the painting.".

a) whose

b) which

c) who

287. Choose the right answer: "Sending ... "special delivery" costs ten times as much as sending it "regular delivery".".

a) mails

b) a piece of mail

c) a mail

288. Choose the right answer: "I was just ... to go out when you telephoned.".

a) about

b) around

c) planned

289. Choose the right answer: "The dentist told him to open his mouth ...".

a) much

b) greatly

c) wide

290. Choose the right answer: "You will spend at least one year working abroad ... you can find out how things operate overseas.".

a) because

b) as long as

c) so that

291. Choose the right answer: "The young girl carefully ... left and right before crossing the road.".

a) looked
b) stared
c) glanced

292. Choose the right answer: "You really can't … a thing that woman says!".
a) rely
b) believe
c) count

293. Choose the right answer: "His house is nothing out of the …; it's just an average three-room house.".
a) ordinary
b) normal
c) usual

294. Choose the right answer: "Swan boat rides provide … from the city's summer heat.".
a) a dismal hiatus
b) a poor relief
c) a restful respite

295. Choose the right answer: "… people can live without any money.".
a) Little
b) Few
c) A little

296. Choose the right answer: "In … cases it is clear who it is that is responsible for a marriage break-up.".
a) few
b) little
c) a little

297. Choose the right answer: "When their mother died, the children were … by their aunt.".
a) brought to
b) brought in
c) brought up

298. Choose the right answer: "I intended to write to you several times, but something was always …".
    a) has interfered
    b) interfered
    c) was interfering

299. Choose the right answer: "He wants to go there and she …".
    a) does either
    b) wants also
    c) does too

300. Choose the right answer: "I should like to become a … of your club.".
    a) member
    b) fellow
    c) associate

Set IV

301. Choose the right answer: "I'm sorry I ... your party.".
    a) lost
    b) missed
    c) passed

302. Choose the right answer: "The workmen made so much ... that I had to spend two days cleaning up afterwards.".
    a) trouble
    b) damage
    c) mess

303. Choose the right answer: "After the game, the referee was interviewed ... television.".
    a) at
    b) on
    c) to

304. Choose the right answer: "He thanked me for what I ... the previous week.".
    a) had done
    b) was doing
    c) did

305. Choose the right answer: "... going to the party.".
    a) Everyone is
    b) Everybody are
    c) Every people is

306. Choose the right answer: "Something extremely strange ... yesterday while we were out jogging.".
    a) was happened
    b) happened
    c) has happened

307. Choose the right answer: "Her English teacher recommends that she ... a regular degree program.".
    a) begins

b) will begin
c) begin

308. Choose the right answer: "How much snow ... now?".
    a) there is
    b) is there
    c) is it

309. Choose the right answer: "The nurse happened to notice the old lady ... to get out of bed.".
    a) to try
    b) trying
    c) tried

310. Choose the right answer: "This morning the postman was ... down the street by my dog.".
    a) chased
    b) run
    c) sped

311. Choose the right answer: "The way he never listens to me really gets ... my nerves.".
    a) up
    b) in
    c) on

312. Choose the right answer: "His speech was not appropriate ... the occasion.".
    a) of
    b) to
    c) with

313. Choose the right answer: "Her parents were very ... because she was out so late that night.".
    a) worried
    b) sorry
    c) overcome

314. Choose the right answer: "If it ..., the match will be postponed.".
    a) will rain

b) rains

c) is raining

315. Choose the right answer: "You look very tired. I ... papers all day.".
	a) had marked
	b) am marking
	c) have been marking

316. Choose the right answer: "When the boy ... the car he was badly injured.".
	a) was hit by
	b) hit
	c) was hitting

317. Choose the right answer: "Monkeys belong to the group of animals ... as primates.".
	a) to know
	b) knowing
	c) known

318. Choose the right answer: "When you do a favour for someone, don't expect anything ...".
	a) in place
	b) instead
	c) in return

319. Choose the right answer: "Since your girlfriend is visiting her family this weekend, ... you like to have dinner with us tonight?".
	a) do
	b) wouldn't
	c) won't

320. Choose the right answer: "How long ... French?".
	a) have you studied
	b) do you study
	c) did you studied

321. Choose the right answer: "My father doesn't work now. He's ... 67.".
	a) over

b) at
c) in

322. Choose the right answer: "Please hurry or you will be late ... school.".
	a) to
	b) at
	c) for

323. Choose the right answer: "The cow had lost its own calf, but the old farmer persuaded it to ... one whose mother had died.".
	a) choose
	b) adopt
	c) collect

324. Choose the right answer: "What's wrong with Daniel? He ... used to be so sad.".
	a) isn't
	b) never
	c) wasn't

325. Choose the right answer: "I'm afraid I've got ... my bank as soon as possible.".
	a) go
	b) going
	c) to go to

326. Choose the right answer: "Tomorrow he will come ... home late.".
	a) -
	b) at
	c) to

327. Choose the right answer: "Ouch! I ... my thumb!".
	a) am to cut
	b) had cut
	c) have cut

328. Choose the right answer: "By then I ... my driving test, I hope.".
	a) pass
	b) will have passed
	c) will be passed

329. Choose the right answer: "I hadn't expected Steve to apologize but I had hoped …".
    a) that he would call me
    b) him calling me
    c) that he call me

330. Choose the right answer: "They always invites my roommate and … to their house.".
    a) my
    b) I
    c) me

331. Choose the right answer: "He was dealt such a severe blow … stunned for several minutes.".
    a) that he was
    b) which caused him to be
    c) so as to make him

332. Choose the right answer: "You will become ill … you stop working so hard.".
    a) when
    b) unless
    c) if

333. Choose the right answer: "I don't think that red dress … her.".
    a) matches
    b) cheers
    c) suits

334. Choose the right answer: "Take this road and you will … at the hotel in ten minutes.".
    a) arrive
    b) find
    c) reach

335. Choose the right answer: "Could you please tell me if you have any electric typewriters …?".
    a) in store
    b) in supply
    c) in stock

336. Choose the right answer: "She sounds very convincing but she's just a fast …".
    a) talker
    b) eyes
    c) ride

337. Choose the right answer: "Mr. Wilson, candidate for governor, was eulogized for his …".
    a) being honest and his loyalty
    b) honesty and courage
    c) wealth and excitement

338. Choose the right answer: "Don't touch that wire or you may get an electric …".
    a) shock
    b) current
    c) feeling

339. Choose the right answer: "A person who says things that are not true is a …".
    a) patient
    b) tailor
    c) liar

340. Choose the right answer: "No matter how hard I tried, he kept on …".
    a) to complain
    b) complaining
    c) complained

341. Choose the right answer: "Can you see the woman … the right?".
    a) off
    b) on
    c) over

342. Choose the right answer: "I still have … time to spare.".
    a) some
    b) much
    c) any

343. Choose the right answer: "This area has a system of … most of which date from the nineteenth century.".
   a) streams
   b) canals
   c) rivers

344. Choose the right answer: "I had quite … on my way to work this morning.".
   a) an affair
   b) a happening
   c) an adventure

345. Choose the right answer: "I think he should … a room in one of the hotels.".
   a) to book
   b) book
   c) booked

346. Choose the right answer: "Would you mind … the window?".
   a) opening
   b) to open
   c) not to open

347. Choose the right answer: "James … me anything about his holiday plans so far.".
   a) don't tell
   b) hasn't told
   c) didn't tell

348. Choose the right answer: "I'm very tired. I … all morning.".
   a) work
   b) have been working
   c) am worked

349. Choose the right answer: "I'd like to know what you do for …".
   a) a job
   b) a profession
   c) a living

350. Choose the right answer: "Daniel didn't come to see the film last night because he ... it before.".
    a) had seen
    b) saw
    c) has seen

351. Choose the right answer: "I ... bacon and eggs every morning.".
    a) am used to eat
    b) am used to eating
    c) use to eat

352. Choose the right answer: "If Brian ... with us, he would have had a good time.".
    a) would come
    b) came
    c) had come

353. Choose the right answer: "I always put my best ... in a safe-deposit box.".
    a) pieces of jewelry
    b) piece of jewelries
    c) jewelries

354. Choose the right answer: "The only way to get ... in this organization is to work hard and make no mistakes.".
    a) with
    b) on
    c) up

355. Choose the right answer: "There are ... leftovers for you in the fridge.".
    a) little
    b) a little
    c) a few

356. Choose the right answer: "Brian is a good student. He always ... his hand.".
    a) raises
    b) rises
    c) arises

357. Choose the right answer: "What will we do today? Let's go for a walk, …?".
   a) do you
   b) shall we
   c) don't you

358. Choose the right answer: "Human beings, as distinct from … animals, can think for themselves.".
   a) another
   b) the others
   c) other

359. Choose the right answer: "The temple is only … drive from the station.".
   a) a few minutes
   b) few minute
   c) a few minute

360. Choose the right answer: "Elementary school children are much more ….than older and more cynical high school students.".
   a) relaxed
   b) trusting
   c) enjoyable

361. Choose the right answer: "Upon hatching, …".
   a) swimming is known by young ducks
   b) young ducks know how to swim
   c) how to swim is known in young ducks

362. Choose the right answer: "Some of the rainwater from clouds evaporates before …".
   a) reaching the ground
   b) to reach the ground
   c) reach the ground

363. Choose the right answer: "The truck … crashed into the back of a bus.".
   a) loading with empty bottles
   b) it was loading with empty bottles
   c) loaded with empty bottles

364. Choose the right answer: "… is entirely up to him.".
    a) He travels
    b) How he travels
    c) How is he traveling

365. Choose the right answer: "… he would have come to class.".
    a) If Daniel is able to finish his homework
    b) Would Daniel be able to finish his homework
    c) If Daniel had been able to finish his homework

366. Choose the right answer: "All of the people at this conference are …".
    a) mathematics teachers
    b) mathematics teacher
    c) mathematic's teachers

367. Choose the right answer: "At an experimental agricultural station, many types of grass are grown … various conditions.".
    a) below
    b) under
    c) beneath

368. Choose the right answer: "… techniques have been developed to diagnose genetic diseases.".
    a) Several of
    b) They are several
    c) Several

369. Choose the right answer: "With new technology, cameras can take pictures of underwater valleys … color.".
    a) in
    b) by
    c) within

370. Choose the right answer: "… are prepared from flour or meal derived from some form of grain.".
    a) With bakery products
    b) Bakery products
    c) They are bakery products

371. Choose the right answer: "... a sizable geographic area, it constitutes a biome.".
   a) A group of plants and animals occupying
   b) That a group of plants and animals occupies
   c) When a group of plants and animals occupies

372. Choose the right answer: "Modern blimps like the famous Goodyear blimps ... the first ones in that they are filled with helium.".
   a) differ from
   b) is different from
   c) different

373. Choose the right answer: "Although Indians fought frequently with the Sioux, they didn't have ... with early white settlers.".
   a) lots contact
   b) much contact
   c) large contact

374. Choose the right answer: "In a hot climate, man acclimatizes by eating less, drinking more liquids, wearing lighter clothing and ...".
   a) skin changes that darken
   b) his skin may darken
   c) experiencing a darkening of the skin

375. Choose the right answer: "Some forms of mollusks are useful as food, especially the bivalves ... oysters, clams and scallops.".
   a) as
   b) such as
   c) so

376. Choose the right answer: "It is now believed that some damage to tissues may result ... them to frequent X-rays.".
   a) from exposing
   b) expose
   c) the exposing

377. Choose the right answer: "These flowers would rather ... in shady places and so would azaleas.".
   a) to grow

b) grown
c) grow

378. Choose the right answer: "Recently, there have been several outbreaks of disease and doctors don't know …".
    a) what the cause is
    b) what is the cause
    c) is what the cause

379. Choose the right answer: "This author, …, spent his boyhood in Arlington.".
    a) was the only child of a high school mathematics teacher
    b) the only child of a high school mathematics teacher
    c) he was the only child of a high school mathematics teacher

380. Choose the right answer: "She entered a university …".
    a) when she had sixteen years
    b) at age sixteen years old
    c) at the age of sixteen

381. Choose the right answer: "The evolution of vertebrates suggests development from a very simple heart in fish to a … in man.".
    a) four-chambers heart
    b) four-chamber heart
    c) four-chamber's heart

382. Choose the right answer: "She didn't know … when his boss called.".
    a) where he was
    b) he was where
    c) where was he

383. Choose the right answer: "Brian's score on the test is the highest in the class; …".
    a) he must had to study last night
    b) he should study last night
    c) he must have studied last night

384. Choose the right answer: "North Carolina is well known not only for the Great Smoky Mountains National Park … for the Cherokee Indian settlements.".

a) because of
b) but also
c) and

385. Choose the right answer: "After the assassination attempt, his doctor suggested that he ... a short rest.".
a) take
b) will take
c) took

386. Choose the right answer: "When sugar ... to yeast, fermentation takes place.".
a) by adding
b) adding
c) is added

387. Choose the right answer: "A good student must know ...".
a) to study hard
b) how to study effectively
c) the way of efficiency in study

388. Choose the right answer: "Daniel was asked to withdraw from graduate school because ...".
a) they believed he was not really able to complete research
b) he was deemed incapable of completing his research
c) it was decided that he was not capable to complete the research

389. Choose the right answer: "Once an offending allergen has been identified ... tests, it is possible for the doctor to give specific desensitizing injections.".
a) means of
b) by means
c) by means of

390. Choose the right answer: "One of hers ... , formed the basis for the newest TV series.".
a) greatest works
b) the greatest work
c) greatest work

391. Choose the right answer: "Not only ... atoms with their microscopes, but they can also make different experiments.".
   a) are today's scientists able to see
   b) able to see today's scientists are
   c) are able to see today's scientists

392. Choose the right answer: "Groups of tissues, each with its own function, ... in the human body.".
   a) they make up the organs
   b) makes up the organs
   c) make up the organs

393. Choose the right answer: "The Immigration Service often ... their visas if they fill out the appropriate papers.".
   a) let students extending
   b) lets students extend
   c) letting students to extend

394. Choose the right answer: "It is necessary ... the approaches to a bridge in such a way as to best accommodate the expected traffic flow over and under it.".
   a) to plan
   b) planning
   c) plan

395. Choose the right answer: "..., the outer layer of the skin, contains pigments, pores and ducts.".
   a) That the epidermis
   b) The epidermis
   c) The epidermis which

396. Choose the right answer: "Rarely ... acorns until the trees are more than twenty years old.".
   a) when oak trees bear
   b) oak trees bear
   c) do oak trees bear

397. Choose the right answer: "Children usually turn to their parents rather than ... for protection from threats.".
   a) to other figures of authority

b) they turn to other figures of authority
c) their turning to other figures of authority

398. Choose the right answer: "Malaria is transmitted by the female, ... by the male mosquito.".
    a) despite
    b) instead
    c) not

399. Choose the right answer: "The Bright University, one of the largest in the nation, is located ... town.".
    a) small midwestern
    b) in a small midwestern
    c) a small midwestern

400. Choose the right answer: "... the best car to buy is a BMW.".
    a) Because of its durability and economy
    b) Because it lasts a long time, and it is very economical
    c) Because of its durability and it is economical

Set V

401. Choose the right answer: "According to some historians, if Napoleon had not invaded Russia, he ... the rest of Europe.".
    a) had conquered
    b) would have conquered
    c) conquered

402. Choose the right answer: "Children learn primarily by ... the world around them.".
    a) experience direct
    b) experiencing directly of
    c) direct physical experience of

403. Choose the right answer: "Partnership is an association of two or more individuals who ... together to develop a business.".
    a) work
    b) they work
    c) working

404. Choose the right answer: "Only when it rains for many days ...".
    a) there a flood is
    b) is there a flood
    c) there is a flood

405. Choose the right answer: "Pre-school students, ..., may be given preferential treatment.".
    a) showing extremely well developed
    b) who show they are extremely well developed
    c) who extremely show well developed

406. Choose the right answer: "... was the day before yesterday.".
    a) The France's Independence Day
    b) French's Independence Day
    c) France's Independence Day

407. Choose the right answer: "The clay burial vessels are decorated with zigzag, grooved and ...".
    a) geometric designs

b) geometry designed

c) geometrically designed

408. Choose the right answer: "… to go to the grocery store every day?".
   a) People in your country like
   b) Have people in your country like
   c) Do people in your country like

409. Choose the right answer: "On this map, the far northern and southern polar regions are …".
   a) great exaggeration in area
   b) greatly exaggerated in area
   c) exaggerating greatly in area

410. Choose the right answer: "Only … of the breeds of cattle have been brought to our country.".
   a) a small amount
   b) a small number
   c) a little amount

411. Choose the right answer: "Chemicals in paint that pose a fire hazard … as combustible, flammable or extremely flammable.".
   a) listed
   b) they are listed
   c) are listed

412. Choose the right answer: "Many books …, but this is one of the best.".
   a) have been written about success
   b) written about success
   c) about successful

413. Choose the right answer: "… a novelty in retailing, fixed prices are now universal in sales.".
   a) That once
   b) Once
   c) It was once

414. Choose the right answer: "… the Gulf Stream is warmer than the ocean water surrounding it.".
   a) Whole

b) A whole as
c) As a whole

415. Choose the right answer: "... heat from the sun is trapped near the earth's surface, the greenhouse effect occurs.".
   a) When
   b) Not
   c) What

416. Choose the right answer: "Drying of meats and vegetables is no longer considered one of ... of preserving food.".
   a) the ways are useful
   b) the most useful ways
   c) most are useful ways

417. Choose the right answer: "... anti-trust laws did not exist, there would not be as much competition in certain industries.".
   a) If
   b) So
   c) Also

418. Choose the right answer: "In 1991 delegates from all countries ... attended the Congress.".
   a) the exception was France
   b) except France
   c) except that France was

419. Choose the right answer: "... Thoreau is known for his transcendental views.".
   a) He was like his predecessor, Emerson,
   b) His predecessor, Emerson, was like him
   c) Like his predecessor, Emerson,

420. Choose the right answer: "When he decided to run for a fourth term, the opposition said that he was ...".
   a) too old
   b) so old
   c) oldest

421. Choose the right answer: "Almost everyone fails … on the first try.".
	a) in passing his driver's test
	b) to pass his driver's test
	c) passing his driver's test

422. Choose the right answer: "This picture … $19.9 million, two times the previous record.".
	a) for sale once
	b) for once sold
	c) once sold for

423. Choose the right answer: "…, human beings have relatively constant body temperature.".
	a) Alike all mammals
	b) Like all mammals
	c) Like all mammal

424. Choose the right answer: "Mr. Adams has not …".
	a) ever lived alone before
	b) never before live sole
	c) lived loneliness in times previous

425. Choose the right answer: "This year will be difficult for this organization because …".
	a) they have less money and volunteers than they had last year
	b) there are fewer money and volunteers that in the last year were
	c) it has less money and fewer volunteers than it had last year

426. Choose the right answer: "The fact that space exploration has increased dramatically in the past thirty years …".
	a) is an evidence of our wanted to know more of our solar system
	b) indicates that we are very eager to learn all we can about our solar system
	c) is pointing to evidence of intention to knowing more about solar systems

427. Choose the right answer: "… is necessary for the development of strong bones and teeth.".
	a) Calcium

b) It is calcium
c) That calcium

428. Choose the right answer: "Frost occurs in valleys and on low grounds ... on adjacent hills.".
    a) frequently than
    b) as frequently than
    c) more frequently than

429. Choose the right answer: "... the fifth largest among the nine planets that make up our solar system.".
    a) The Earth is
    b) The Earth being
    c) Being the Earth

430. Choose the right answer: "Only rarely ... neuroses leave a person unable to function in everyday situations.".
    a) had
    b) do
    c) are

431. Choose the right answer: "Anxiety about uncontrollable situations is thought to cause ...".
    a) fitful in sleep
    b) sleep fitfully
    c) fitful sleep

432. Choose the right answer: "Most stores in large America cities close ... five or six o'clock.".
    a) in
    b) at
    c) on

433. Choose the right answer: "About half of the children in America must ... in single-parent homes.".
    a) grow up
    b) to grow up
    c) growing up

434. Choose the right answer: "… is an ancient source of energy.".
    a) The wind
    b) A wind
    c) Wind

435. Choose the right answer: "Charlie Chaplin was a comedian … was best known for his work in silent movies.".
    a) which
    b) who
    c) what

436. Choose the right answer: "In a parliamentary system, it is not the monarch but the prime minister …".
    a) who has the real power
    b) whom the real power
    c) who the real power

437. Choose the right answer: "Geomorphology is the study of the changes that … on the surface of the earth.".
    a) taking place
    b) they take place
    c) take place

438. Choose the right answer: "In this country … picturesque fishing villages and manufacturing towns.".
    a) has
    b) there are
    c) many

439. Choose the right answer: "… all citrus fruit originated with the Chinese orange.".
    a) It is believed that
    b) The belief that
    c) To believe that

440. Choose the right answer: "Most people don't object … them by their first names.".
    a) that I call
    b) to my calling
    c) for calling

441. Choose the right answer: "The politician was impressed with Lincoln … he found him entirely free of prejudice.".
    a) because
    b) who
    c) therefore

442. Choose the right answer: "Perspiration increases … vigorous exercise or hot weather.".
    a) when
    b) for
    c) during

443. Choose the right answer: "He told us … one man and six women applying for the job.".
    a) it was
    b) there is
    c) there was

444. Choose the right answer: "The doctor was worried about the patient because she appeared listless and …".
    a) pale
    b) weak
    c) spirit

445. Choose the right answer: "They decided to finish and finally … the evening with a pizza and a few sodas.".
    a) terminate
    b) enjoy
    c) end

446. Choose the right answer: "Employers often require that candidates have not only a degree in engineering …".
    a) also two years experience
    b) but more two years experience
    c) but also two years experience

447. Choose the right answer: "Prices for bikes can run … $2.500.".
    a) as high as
    b) so high to
    c) so high as

448. Choose the right answer: "... 100 species of finch have been identified.".
- a) Much as
- b) As many as
- c) As many

449. Choose the right answer: "It can sometimes ... a home.".
- a) to take months to sell
- b) take several months to sell
- c) to sell taking several months

450. Choose the right answer: "... the coming of autumn, thousands of tourists follow the ridge trail to observe the autumnal foliage.".
- a) When
- b) As soon as
- c) With

451. Choose the right answer: "... two and one half hours to climb to the top of this mountain.".
- a) To take it typically
- b) It typically takes
- c) Typically takes it

452. Choose the right answer: "Although exact statistics vary because of political changes, ... separate nation states are included in this list.".
- a) more than two hundred
- b) many that two hundred
- c) as much as two hundred

453. Choose the right answer: "The yearly path of the sun around the heavens ...".
- a) it is known to be ecliptic
- b) knowing as the ecliptic
- c) is known as the ecliptic

454. Choose the right answer: "According to a recent survey, ... doctors do not have a personal physician.".
- a) large number of
- b) a large number of
- c) large amount of

455. Choose the right answer: "The tiny pictures on microfilm are … small to be read with the naked eye.".
    a) too
    b) so
    c) such

456. Choose the right answer: "Memorial Day is usually celebrated on …".
    a) May thirty
    b) the thirtieth of May
    c) thirtieth May

457. Choose the right answer: "This volcano … on the eastern slope.".
    a) situating
    b) to situate
    c) is situated

458. Choose the right answer: "The sudden expansion of heated air associated with lightning produces … often heard during a storm.".
    a) thunder, the rumbling sound
    b) the rumbling sound, thunder is
    c) the rumbling sound, thunder, that

459. Choose the right answer: "…, business managers plan the tasks that their employees are to carry out.".
    a) They process the organizing
    b) Through the organizing process
    c) While the organizing process

460. Choose the right answer: "A child in the first grade tends to be … all of the other children in his class.".
    a) the same age as
    b) as old like
    c) the same old to

461. Choose the right answer: "Brian contributed fifty dollars, but he wishes he could contribute …".
    a) one other fifty dollars
    b) the same amount also
    c) another fifty

462. Choose the right answer: "It is gravity ... objects toward the earth.".
    a) that pulls
    b) pulling
    c) to pull

463. Choose the right answer: "Using a globe can be ... it is educational.".
    a) enjoyable
    b) as enjoyable as
    c) to enjoy as

464. Choose the right answer: "Many people ... to California for gold in 1848.".
    a) rushed
    b) rushing
    c) are rushed

465. Choose the right answer: "... many of the designs for the new capital were considered lost forever, he helped reproduce the original plans.".
    a) During
    b) How
    c) When

466. Choose the right answer: "The wheel, ... has remained important for more than 4000 years, is one of mankind's first inventions.".
    a) when
    b) which
    c) how

467. Choose the right answer: "... has improved a lot since she started her new job.".
    a) To type like Sarah
    b) Sarah's typing
    c) Sarah types

468. Choose the right answer: "I know ... a different way to get there but I like this one.".
    a) there is
    b) that is
    c) it is

469. Choose the right answer: "Physical fitness exercises can cause injuries ... the participants are not careful.".
    a) that
    b) with
    c) if

470. Choose the right answer: "Although solar energy is cheaper than oil, ... have advantages as well as disadvantages.".
    a) so both
    b) both of them
    c) the two

471. Choose the right answer: "Birds head south to warmer climates when ...".
    a) comes cold weather
    b) is cold weather
    c) cold weather comes

472. Choose the right answer: "If one of the participants in a conversation wonders ..., no real communication has taken place.".
    a) what the other person said
    b) what said the other person
    c) what was the other person say

473. Choose the right answer: "He ... looked forward to the new venture.".
    a) with great eagerness
    b) eagerly
    c) in a state of increasing eagerness

474. Choose the right answer: "The juice contained in the brittles of the nettle causes an intense itch when ... a persons skin.".
    a) its entry in
    b) it enters
    c) there it enters

475. Choose the right answer: "Everyone ... albinos has a certain amount of pigment in the skin to add color.".
    a) but
    b) that
    c) not

476. Choose the right answer: "The Congress granted federal lands to the states ... agricultural and mechanical arts colleges.".
    a) establish
    b) establishment
    c) to establish

477. Choose the right answer: "Ancient people believed that ... with a sun and a moon rotating around it.".
    a) the earth was the center of the universe
    b) the center of the universe is earth
    c) the universe has earth at the center

478. Choose the right answer: "Technically, glass is a mineral and ...".
    a) water so
    b) so is water
    c) so water is

479. Choose the right answer: "Unlike the earth, which rotates once every twenty-four hours, ... once every ten hours.".
    a) Jupiter rotates
    b) the rotation of Jupiter
    c) Jupiter's rotating

480. Choose the right answer: "They were happy the train arrived on time and ...".
    a) punctually
    b) not late at all
    c) at the right platform

481. Choose the right answer: "... a teacher in Spain, she wrote a dictionary.".
    a) While
    b) It was while
    c) When

482. Choose the right answer: "About 10 kilometers from the capital, ... a little town named Dantom that has a rich history.".
    a) has
    b) there is
    c) where is

483. Choose the right answer: "... the promotion of health and to helping people avoid injury and disease.".
　　a) To commit the Red Cross
　　b) Committed to the Red Cross is
　　c) The Red Cross is committed to

484. Choose the right answer: "The bank ... the bookstore has been broken into.".
　　a) across from
　　b) between
　　c) at

485. Choose the right answer: "It was not until she had arrived home ... remembered her appointment with the doctor.".
　　a) when she
　　b) that she
　　c) and she

486. Choose the right answer: "Several of these washers and dryers are out of order and ...".
　　a) need to be repaired
　　b) need to be repairing
　　c) repairing is required of them

487. Choose the right answer: "If it hadn't been for the war, probably the unemployment rate of 15% ... still further.".
　　a) would rise
　　b) would have risen
　　c) had risen

488. Choose the right answer: "They tried to nominate him for the Presidency ...".
　　a) when he had only twenty-eight years
　　b) at age twenty-eight years
　　c) when he was only twenty-eight

489. Choose the right answer: "Not only knowledge and skills, but also attitudes ... in school.".
　　a) need to be cultivated

b) cultivated
c) when cultivated

490. Choose the right answer: "… west of the Rocky Mountains.".
a) Never tornadoes almost occur
b) Tornadoes almost never occur
c) Tornadoes never occurs almost

491. Choose the right answer: "Vitamins are organic compounds …".
a) not produced them by the body
b) the body can't produce them
c) that can't be produced by the body

492. Choose the right answer: "Seals can … because they have a thick layer of blubber.".
a) keep themselves warm
b) keep them warm
c) keep their warm

493. Choose the right answer: "This story, written about 1432, is alive and … today as it was nearly 600 years ago.".
a) appealed
b) the appeal of
c) appealing

494. Choose the right answer: "Each of the radioisotopes produced artificially … its own distinct structure.".
a) having
b) has
c) have had

495. Choose the right answer: "This tale is a mythical account of evil and revenge as shown by the hero's pursuit of the whale that had wounded … earlier in life.".
a) him
b) he
c) to him

496. Choose the right answer: "In a suspension bridge … that carry one or more flexible cables firmly attached at each end.".

a) towers there are two
   b) there are two towers
   c) there is two towers on it

497. Choose the right answer: "The derby ... every May.".
   a) it may be run
   b) is run
   c) to be run

498. Choose the right answer: "The nuthatch ... six inches long.".
   a) grows seldom more than
   b) grows more than seldom
   c) seldom grows more than

499. Choose the right answer: "The Andromeda Nebula, ... more than two million light years away, can be seen from the northern hemisphere.".
   a) a galaxy
   b) is a galaxy
   c) a galaxy which

500. Choose the right answer: "Sarah will wash the clothes, ...".
   a) iron the shirts, prepare the meal and dust the furniture
   b) iron the shirts, prepare the meal, dusting the furniture
   c) ironing the shirts, preparing the meal and dusting the furniture

Set VI

501. Choose the right answer: "It has been estimated that … one hundred thousand men participated in the gold rush.".
    a) approximate
    b) as many as
    c) more

502. Choose the right answer: "A sixteen-year-old is not … to vote in an election.".
    a) as old enough
    b) enough old
    c) old enough

503. Choose the right answer: "As soon as … with an acid, salt and sometimes water, is formed.".
    a) a base reacts
    b) a base will react
    c) a base is reacting

504. Choose the right answer: "The theater where Lincoln was shot …".
    a) must restore
    b) must restored
    c) must have been restored

505. Choose the right answer: "The skiers would rather … through the mountains than go by bus.".
    a) to travel on train
    b) travel by train
    c) traveling by the train

506. Choose the right answer: "She has received several scholarships …".
    a) because of her academic and the artistic ability
    b) not only because of her artistic but her academic ability
    c) as a resulting of her ability in the art and the academy

507. Choose the right answer: "The medical doctor insisted that his patient …".
    a) taking it easy inside of three months

  b) take it easy for three months
  c) to take some vacations for three months

508. Choose the right answer: "Legumes take nitrogen into their roots … the air.".
  a) but
  b) except
  c) from

509. Choose the right answer: "So little … that he failed the examination.".
  a) knew the student
  b) did the student know
  c) the student had known

510. Choose the right answer: "The belief in life after death is prevalent in both primitive societies … advanced cultures.".
  a) and
  b) and in
  c) also

511. Choose the right answer: "Copper is the favored metal for electricians' wire because of …".
  a) its excellent conductivity
  b) it is an excellent conductor
  c) so conductive is it

512. Choose the right answer: "Before the Angles … to England, the Iberians had lived there.".
  a) come
  b) did come
  c) came

513. Choose the right answer: "A bookstore that sells used textbooks stocks … along with the new ones on the shelf under the course title.".
  a) its
  b) them
  c) their

514. Choose the right answer: "… discovery of insulin, it was not possible to treat diabetes.".

a) Prior to the
b) The prior
c) Prior

515. Choose the right answer: "Out of this book ... for an increase in public goods, potentially at the expense of private goods.".
   a) argued
   b) came the argument
   c) his argument

516. Choose the right answer: "The human body has four jugular veins, ... each side of the neck.".
   a) there are two on
   b) two are on
   c) two on

517. Choose the right answer: "When ... of impulses from many neurons in one part of the brain, an epileptic seizure occurs.".
   a) there are simultaneous bursts
   b) the simultaneous bursts
   c) simultaneously bursting

518. Choose the right answer: "Aspirin is used ... a constriction of the blood vessels.".
   a) counteracting
   b) counteract
   c) to counteract

519. Choose the right answer: "... gene in the human genome were more completely understood, many diseases could be cured or prevented.".
   a) Since each
   b) If each
   c) Were each

520. Choose the right answer: "Only after food has been dried or canned ...".
   a) should it be stored for later consumption
   b) that it should be stored for later consumption
   c) it should be stored for later consumption

521. Choose the right answer: "In …, the advent of the telephone, radio and internet has made rapid long-distance communication possible.".
 a) one hundred years later
 b) the last one hundred years
 c) the one hundred years since

522. Choose the right answer: "… people came to the meeting than we had expected.".
 a) Fewer
 b) Less
 c) Little

523. Choose the right answer: "Art lovers should read … about what new paintings will be displayed.".
 a) noticing
 b) noticeably
 c) notices

524. Choose the right answer: "The committee has met and …".
 a) it has reached a decision
 b) its decision was reached at
 c) they have reached a decision

525. Choose the right answer: "This cathedral enjoys the distinction … the largest medieval cathedral in the world.".
 a) to be
 b) of being
 c) it being

526. Choose the right answer: "Our professor is not only a successful novelist, … an expert linguist.".
 a) however
 b) but also
 c) and also

527. Choose the right answer: "The organization has been in existence … 1920.".
 a) starting in
 b) after
 c) since

528. Choose the right answer: "One of the puzzles still mystifying biologists is ... what to become in an embryo.".
- a) how cells know
- b) how cells knowing
- c) how do cells know

529. Choose the right answer: "The man gave ... a diamond necklace.".
- a) that is his wife
- b) it to his wife
- c) his wife

530. Choose the right answer: "Steve has not been able to recall where ...".
- a) she lives
- b) does she live
- c) did she live

531. Choose the right answer: "Depressant drugs ... historically have been known to be addictive are called narcotics.".
- a) and
- b) which
- c) about which

532. Choose the right answer: "If Americans ate fewer foods with sugar and salt, their general health ... better.".
- a) be
- b) is
- c) would be

533. Choose the right answer: "At this five-and-ten-cent store, ... more than a dime.".
- a) no item cost
- b) items not cost
- c) neither items cost

534. Choose the right answer: "... the end of the Ice Age, mammoths became extinct.".
- a) It was
- b) With
- c) That

535. Choose the right answer: "There are two basic kinds of air compressors, reciprocating and …".
	a) one that rotates
	b) a rotating kind
	c) rotating

536. Choose the right answer: "Daniel Smith, a novelist, … about a restless man's quest for inner peace.".
	a) wrote
	b) who wrote
	c) who wrote this

537. Choose the right answer: "…, the jaguar used to roam freely in the southwestern United States.".
	a) To being found in Central and South America
	b) Now found only in Central and South America
	c) It is now found only in Central and South America

538. Choose the right answer: "When linguists encounter a new language, … work to identify all of the sounds it contains.".
	a) those
	b) who
	c) they

539. Choose the right answer: "Air … the carbon dioxide necessary for photosynthesis enters leaves through tiny surface openings.".
	a) contains
	b) containing
	c) it contains

540. Choose the right answer: "Steven did not do well in the class because …".
	a) he failed to study properly
	b) he studied bad
	c) he was a badly student

541. Choose the right answer: "In his autobiography, the author attempted to show that his generation …".
	a) did not know living in a technological society

b) did not know how to live in a technological society

c) had not known living in a technological society

542. Choose the right answer: "We all saw the athlete when he … the fastest kilometer ever run at the school.".

    a) running

    b) run

    c) ran

543. Choose the right answer: "The … wanted to continue their tour even though the car had broken down.".

    a) tourists have

    b) tourists

    c) tourist had

544. Choose the right answer: "For the investor who … money, silver or bonds are good options.".

    a) has very little

    b) has so few

    c) has very few

545. Choose the right answer: "To relieve pain caused by burns, prevent infection and treat shocks, …".

    a) take immediate steps

    b) to take immediate steps

    c) taking immediate steps

546. Choose the right answer: "This country doesn't require European citizens obtain passports to enter it, and …".

    a) either does Mexico

    b) neither Mexico does

    c) Mexico doesn't either

547. Choose the right answer: "Flight fifteen from Spain to Portugal is now arriving at …".

    a) the gate two

    b) gate two

    c) the two gate

548. Choose the right answer: "Sesame … a herbaceous plant native to the tropics.".
    a) which
    b) is
    c) from

549. Choose the right answer: "A log grabber has a long arm …, which stretches out to pick up logs.".
    a) called a jib
    b) calls a jib
    c) a jib called

550. Choose the right answer: "The families were told to evacuate their houses immediately …".
    a) in the time when the water raised
    b) when up was going the water
    c) when the water began to rise

551. Choose the right answer: "… the lip of an open-pit copper mine, the huge tractors and cranes look like toys.".
    a) Where
    b) From
    c) That

552. Choose the right answer: "Double starts orbit …".
    a) each other
    b) each to the other
    c) other each one

553. Choose the right answer: "The bird's egg is such an efficient structure for protecting the embryo inside … difficult to be broken.".
    a) that
    b) and is
    c) that it is

554. Choose the right answer: "Besides rain, … is seldom pure.".
    a) natural water
    b) water naturally
    c) water of nature

555. Choose the right answer: "A dolphin ... a porpoise in that it has a longer nose.".
    a) differs
    b) different than
    c) differs from

556. Choose the right answer: "The Olympic flame burns ... throughout the games.".
    a) continuously
    b) continual
    c) in a continuous way

557. Choose the right answer: "Corn is not native to America and winter wheat ...".
    a) is either
    b) isn't either
    c) is neither

558. Choose the right answer: "Although blood ... a residue in urine and stool samples, it cannot be detected without a microscope.".
    a) let
    b) lets
    c) leaves

559. Choose the right answer: "Prospectors rushed to this area in 1956 ... was discovered here.".
    a) after gold soon
    b) soon after gold
    c) they found gold

560. Choose the right answer: "... the Christmas shopping season begins.".
    a) It is after Thanksgiving that
    b) After Thanksgiving it is
    c) That is after Thanksgiving

561. Choose the right answer: "The plant is ... big that it should really be moved outside.".
    a) so
    b) such
    c) very

562. Choose the right answer: "People should have ... as their desires will allow.".
    a) education
    b) for education
    c) as much education

563. Choose the right answer: "... strength of 50 horses, a forklift lifts great weights.".
    a) With the
    b) Some
    c) Because the

564. Choose the right answer: "The shoe-lasting machine ... production but it also cut the cost of shoe production by half.".
    a) increased only
    b) not only increased
    c) only have increased

565. Choose the right answer: "This man developed the first rocket to fly faster ...".
    a) than sound is
    b) than sound
    c) does sound

566. Choose the right answer: "Some students are frightened the university ... tuition fees to meet the rise in the cost of living.".
    a) raise
    b) raising
    c) will raise

567. Choose the right answer: "It is very difficult to stop the cultivation of marijuana because ...".
    a) it grows well with little care
    b) it grows very carelessly
    c) it doesn't care much to grow

568. Choose the right answer: "Automobile production in the European Union ...".
    a) has been erratically lately

b) are going up and down all the time

c) has been rather erratic recently

569. Choose the right answer: "On the slope of that peak in Colorado ... the ruin of a gigantic tree.".

    a) where lies

    b) lies

    c) lie

570. Choose the right answer: "... that the English settled in this town.".

    a) It was in 1709

    b) That in 1709

    c) Because in 1709

571. Choose the right answer: "Agronomists work to improve the quality of crops, increase the yield of fields and ... of the soil.".

    a) maintaining the quality

    b) the quality is maintained

    c) maintain the quality

572. Choose the right answer: "Nitric acid ... copper to give off brown fumes of nitrogen dioxide.".

    a) reacts with

    b) on reacting with

    c) is reacting with

573. Choose the right answer: "Although the name was not popularized, engineering ... civilization.".

    a) as old as

    b) that is old as

    c) is as old as

574. Choose the right answer: "Penguins may live ... twenty years.".

    a) before

    b) for

    c) from

575. Choose the right answer: "A desert receives less than twenty-five ... of rainfall every year.".

    a) centimeters

b) a centimeter
c) of centimeters

576. Choose the right answer: "Most beekeepers have observed … at the approach of a thunderstorm.".
    a) become enraged the bees
    b) that bees enraging
    c) that bees become enraged

577. Choose the right answer: "The jaw structure of a snake permits it to eat and digest animals much larger than …".
    a) its
    b) itself
    c) it has

578. Choose the right answer: "When a woman becomes pregnant … in life, she encounters additional risks in delivering a healthy baby.".
    a) late
    b) latest
    c) lately

579. Choose the right answer: "… of Western singers may be related to old English ballads.".
    a) The music
    b) Music
    c) Their music

580. Choose the right answer: "The United States is … that there are five time zones.".
    a) too big
    b) very big
    c) so big

581. Choose the right answer: "Mr. Smith doesn't know … the lawn mower after they had finished using it.".
    a) where they put
    b) where to put
    c) where did they put

582. Choose the right answer: "The painting ... to the art museum last week.".
    a) donated
    b) was donated
    c) donating

583. Choose the right answer: "Because he was feeling unwell, ... to miss the examination.".
    a) that he wanted
    b) wanted
    c) the student wanted

584. Choose the right answer: "... cheaper, she would have bought it.".
    a) The laptop
    b) Had the laptop been
    c) If the laptop is

585. Choose the right answer: "The most noticeable feature of African elephants ... their large ears being quite different from the ears of Asian ones.".
    a) with
    b) are
    c) is

586. Choose the right answer: "My yearly income since I changed professions has ...".
    a) nearly tripled
    b) got almost three times bigger
    c) just about gone up three times

587. Choose the right answer: "Although the weather in my vineyard isn't ... to have a year round tourist season, it has become a favorite summer resort.".
    a) goodly enough
    b) good enough
    c) enough good

588. Choose the right answer: "Sound comes in waves, and the higher the frequency, ...".
    a) pitch is the higher

b) higher is the pitch
c) the higher the pitch

589. Choose the right answer: "It was proposed by the new member on the committee that membership fees … reduced.".
    a) be
    b) will be
    c) can be

590. Choose the right answer: "Neither Sarah nor her brothers … a consent form.".
    a) need
    b) is needing
    c) has need

591. Choose the right answer: "Trace minerals are … are elements needed in greater quantities.".
    a) most important to healthy human tissue
    b) important to healthy human tissue
    c) as important to healthy human tissue as

592. Choose the right answer: "The director was angry because somebody …".
    a) had allowed the photographers to enter the building
    b) permitting the photographers enter the building
    c) the photographers let into the building

593. Choose the right answer: "He had been a lawyer and … before he entered politics.".
    a) served in the Navy as an officer
    b) an officer in the Navy
    c) did service in the Navy as an officer

594. Choose the right answer: "The two main … are permanent magnets and electromagnets.".
    a) kind of magnets
    b) kinds of magnet
    c) kinds of magnets

595. Choose the right answer: "There are few beautifully preserved buildings …".
   a) on Beacon Street
   b) in Beacon Street
   c) at Beacon Street

596. Choose the right answer: "Clones, …, are genetically homogenous.".
   a) plant growing from a single specimen
   b) plants grown from a single specimen
   c) that a plant grown from a single specimen

597. Choose the right answer: "Although scientists had hoped that interferon … to be a cure for cancer, its applications now appear to be more limited.".
   a) prove
   b) will prove
   c) would prove

598. Choose the right answer: "… his life, this author was regarded as the foremost American novelist.".
   a) During
   b) While
   c) By the time of

599. Choose the right answer: "… born, a baby kangaroo measures about five centimeters in length.".
   a) One is
   b) When it is
   c) When is one

600. Choose the right answer: "Electron storage rings … in investigations of the structure of materials.".
   a) used
   b) they are used
   c) are used

Set VII

601. Choose the right answer: "It is generally true that the lower the stock market falls, …".
    a) higher the price of gold rises
    b) the higher the price of gold rises
    c) rises high the price of gold

602. Choose the right answer: "Because aluminum is lighter and cheaper …, it is used for high-tension power transmission.".
    a) than copper
    b) as copper
    c) for copper

603. Choose the right answer: "This mountain … to a height of 13,484 feet.".
    a) soared
    b) soaring
    c) soars

604. Choose the right answer: "A good teaching technique for … students active is group work.".
    a) to keep
    b) kept
    c) keeping

605. Choose the right answer: "Isaac Newton, …, made his discoveries about gravity a long time ago.".
    a) an English scientist and philosopher
    b) was an English scientist and philosopher
    c) being an English scientist and philosopher

606. Choose the right answer: "He would certainly have attended the proceedings …".
    a) if he didn't get the flat tire
    b) had he not had a flat tire
    c) if his flat tire hadn't happened

607. Choose the right answer: "Ancient civilizations … goods rather than use money.".

a) use to trade
b) used to trade
c) was used to trade

608. Choose the right answer: "The television programs we allow ... to watch influence their learning.".
a) a children
b) their child
c) our children

609. Choose the right answer: "She lost her sight and hearing after a severe illness ...".
a) when she was 19 months old
b) of her age in 19 months
c) she was 19 months old

610. Choose the right answer: "The most exact way known to science ... the age of artifacts is based on the radioactivity.".
a) for to determine
b) for determining
c) to determining

611. Choose the right answer: "He has used what he learned ... to produce taped oral histories.".
a) when he was a radio talk show host
b) a radio talk show host
c) when was he a radio talk show host

612. Choose the right answer: "One of the least effective ways of storing information is learning ... it.".
a) how repeat
b) repeat
c) to repeat

613. Choose the right answer: "The theory of Continental Drift assumes that there ... long-term climatic changes in many areas during the past.".
a) must be
b) must have
c) must have been

614. Choose the right answer: "Water is ... that is generally contains dissolved materials.".
   a) a such excellent solvent
   b) such an excellent solvent
   c) such a excellent solvents

615. Choose the right answer: "From 2000 until her death, Mary ... the National Museum of Natural History.".
   a) was associated with
   b) associates with
   c) is associated with

616. Choose the right answer: "The novel, ..., is set in Europe.".
   a) was written by Mr. Buck
   b) which was written by Mr. Buck
   c) which by Mr. Buck

617. Choose the right answer: "In medieval times ... his enemy to fight by throwing down his gauntlet.".
   a) the challenge
   b) his challenge
   c) a man challenged

618. Choose the right answer: "Although most cats hate to swim, ... if necessary.".
   a) they can do so
   b) so can they do
   c) can they to do

619. Choose the right answer: "Scientists believe that the beaver's instinct to build dams is more complex than ... other animal instinct.".
   a) most
   b) these
   c) any

620. Choose the right answer: "The general manager usually ... unless his press secretary approves it.".
   a) no statement
   b) doesn't make a statement
   c) doesn't statement

621. Choose the right answer: "The fuel used in nuclear-powered ships is usually uranium in either the metallic ...".
    a) as well as the oxide form
    b) and the oxide form
    c) or the oxide form

622. Choose the right answer: "The bank manager advised him ... his savings into a time deposit account.".
    a) to put
    b) put
    c) putting

623. Choose the right answer: "She bought a ... on sale.".
    a) stereo complete system
    b) complete stereo system
    c) stereo system complete

624. Choose the right answer: "She bought ... fruit because so many people were coming to visit.".
    a) as much
    b) very much
    c) many

625. Choose the right answer: "Mr. Smith will not be able to attend the meeting tonight because ...".
    a) he will be teaching a class
    b) of he ill teach a class
    c) he must to teach a class

626. Choose the right answer: "The teachers have had some problems deciding ...".
    a) the time when the final papers they should return for the students
    b) when to the students they shall return the final papers
    c) when they should return the final papers to the students

627. Choose the right answer: "Violence on campuses has abated ...".
    a) after 1950
    b) since 1950
    c) for 1950

628. Choose the right answer: "General Smith had the officer ... him at this hill.".
   a) meet
   b) to meet
   c) meeting

629. Choose the right answer: "People usually can get a sufficient amount of the calcium their bodies ... from the food they consume.".
   a) needing
   b) need
   c) to need

630. Choose the right answer: "Fast-food restaurants have become popular because many working people want ...".
   a) eat quickly and cheaply
   b) the eat quickly and cheap
   c) to eat quickly and cheaply

631. Choose the right answer: "Small microcomputers of today can process ... their predecessors, which were many times their size.".
   a) the same amount of information as
   b) in the same amount of information
   c) and have the same amount of information

632. Choose the right answer: "There were two small rooms in the beach house, ... served as a kitchen.".
   a) smallest of that
   b) the smaller of which
   c) the smaller of them

633. Choose the right answer: "The bodies of living creatures are organized into many different systems, each of which has ... function.".
   a) a certain
   b) certainly
   c) to be certain

634. Choose the right answer: "One's fingerprints are ...".
   a) different from any other person
   b) differs from another person
   c) different from those of any other person

635. Choose the right answer: "... of the country a vast urban region has been established.".
    a) That the northeastern seaboard
    b) On the northeastern seaboard
    c) It is the northeastern seaboard

636. Choose the right answer: "Some plants are annuals; ... are biennials; the rest are perennials.".
    a) some another
    b) others
    c) other

637. Choose the right answer: "The giraffe survives because it ... the vegetation in the high branches.".
    a) can reach
    b) to reach
    c) reach

638. Choose the right answer: "By throwing rocks in saloon windows and destroying saloons, ...".
    a) alcohol was prohibited by her
    b) she worked to prohibit alcohol
    c) prohibiting alcohol by her

639. Choose the right answer: "The anthropologist ... that witchcraft beliefs are prevalent in these societies.".
    a) was found
    b) finding
    c) found

640. Choose the right answer: "When a body enters the earth's atmosphere, it travels ...".
    a) very rapidly
    b) fastly
    c) with greed speed

641. Choose the right answer: "... Giant Ape Man was just about the size of a male gorilla.".
    a) That it is

b) That believing
c) It is believed that

642. Choose the right answer: "The strongest trucks work in rock quarries, ... tons of rocks and soil at one time.".
   a) that they move
   b) where they move
   c) they move

643. Choose the right answer: "Poison oak generates irritating poisons ... even if people merely brush against the plants.".
   a) that can affect people
   b) what can effect people
   c) which do they affect

644. Choose the right answer: "The mechanic told the car owner that he should not ... the car over 70 kilometers per hour.".
   a) have drive
   b) drive
   c) driving

645. Choose the right answer: "The committee decided to award ... a prize even though she didn't win.".
   a) she
   b) her the contestant
   c) the contestant

646. Choose the right answer: "... the last lunar eclipse lasting longer than any this century, we were able to try out our new telescope.".
   a) During
   b) While
   c) As

647. Choose the right answer: "Since her father never approved of ... Daniel, the couple eloped to Spain where they lived and wrote.".
   a) her to marry
   b) she to marry
   c) her marrying

648. Choose the right answer: "Not until the mid-nineteenth century ... achieve recognition.".
    a) did her work
    b) had her work
    c) her work

649. Choose the right answer: "... their territories but rather than fight, they howl.".
    a) Jealous of wolves
    b) Wolves jealously protect
    c) Protection of wolves

650. Choose the right answer: "The TOEFL examination ... by the tear 2020.".
    a) is revised completely
    b) is to be revised completely
    c) completely revised

651. Choose the right answer: "This man revolutionized production management by ... into small steps on a moving line.".
    a) breaking down auto assembly
    b) he broke down auto assembly
    c) auto assembly breaking down

652. Choose the right answer: "Unemployment compensation is money to support an unemployed person while he or she is looking for ...".
    a) work
    b) a job
    c) works

653. Choose the right answer: "Many chemicals react ... in acid solutions.".
    a) more quick
    b) as quickly more
    c) more quickly

654. Choose the right answer: "She collected many beautiful antiques and ... them among the original pieces in the house.".
    a) set
    b) sit
    c) sat

655. Choose the right answer: "Of all the cities in this country, …".
    a) this is probably the most picturesque
    b) that this city if probably the most picturesque
    c) this city is probably the most picturesque

656. Choose the right answer: "… peaches are classified as freestone or clingstone depends on how difficult it is to remove the pit.".
    a) About
    b) Whether
    c) The

657. Choose the right answer: "This is … poisonous lizards found in this area.".
    a) one of the few
    b) few
    c) the one

658. Choose the right answer: "… cockroach is the pest most in need of eradication is generally agreed upon.".
    a) The
    b) It is the
    c) That the

659. Choose the right answer: "The flamingo uses its bill … feeding to filter mud and water.".
    a) when
    b) that it is
    c) was

660. Choose the right answer: "Researchers have recently confirmed … Pygmies are missing a growth factor.".
    a) so that
    b) that
    c) because

661. Choose the right answer: "… and the Japanese crested ibis are among the most endangered birds.".
    a) The Marianas mallard
    b) There are the Marianas mallard
    c) Being the Marianas mallard

662. Choose the right answer: "The boy was ashamed ... he had broken the window.".
    a) admitted
    b) admit
    c) to admit

663. Choose the right answer: "She said she didn't like ...".
    a) shop
    b) shopping
    c) when shopping

664. Choose the right answer: "Into the Bermuda Triangle ..., never to be seen again.".
    a) sailed the ship
    b) the ship sailed
    c) to sail the ship

665. Choose the right answer: "Nobody really knew the ... solution.".
    a) better
    b) good
    c) best

666. Choose the right answer: "The residents of the building ...".
    a) sent faithfully flowers all weeks to the cemetery
    b) sent flowers faithfully to the cemetery each week
    c) sent each week faithfully to the cemetery flowers

667. Choose the right answer: "The students like that professor's course because ...".
    a) not a lot of homework
    b) there was little or no homework
    c) of there wasn't a great amount of homework

668. Choose the right answer: "To answer accurately is more important than ...".
    a) to finish quickly
    b) a quick finish
    c) you finish quickly

669. Choose the right answer: "An advisor to both Smith and Mark, ... of this College.".
    a) Dr. Adams was the founder
    b) the founder was Dr. Adams
    c) did the founder Dr. Adams

670. Choose the right answer: "By observing rapid eye movements, ... to know when dreaming occurs during sleep.".
    a) then is possible
    b) it is the possibility
    c) it is possible

671. Choose the right answer: "... up to six months.".
    a) Lasting New England winters
    b) The length of a New England winter
    c) New England winters can last

672. Choose the right answer: "..., he would have been able to pass the exam.".
    a) Had he studied more
    b) If studied more
    c) Studying more

673. Choose the right answer: "It is important that the IELTS Office ... an applicant's registration.".
    a) will confirm
    b) conform
    c) must confirm

674. Choose the right answer: "A good team ... of both recruiting and coaching as well as performing.".
    a) result it
    b) are a result
    c) resulting

675. Choose the right answer: "The first transistor was a small chip made of germanium onto one surface of which two pointed wire contacts ... side by side.".
    a) were made

b) making

c) made

676. Choose the right answer: "Ladybugs help farmers by …".
   a) eat other insects
   b) other insect's eating
   c) eating other insects

677. Choose the right answer: "To check for acidity, one had better … litmus paper.".
   a) use
   b) using
   c) useful

678. Choose the right answer: "A thermometer is an instrument that … temperature.".
   a) the heat
   b) measures
   c) does not

679. Choose the right answer: "… cause extensive damage to these nations each year.".
   a) Because of high tides and winds
   b) That the high tides and winds of hurricanes
   c) The high tides and winds of hurricanes

680. Choose the right answer: "… two waves pass a given point simultaneously, they will have no effect on each other's.".
   a) If
   b) They are
   c) So that

681. Choose the right answer: "Mark belongs to the …".
   a) class of the upper middle
   b) upper middle class
   c) high medium class

682. Choose the right answer: "Alison, … to head the marketing department at age 28, is one of the youngest college.".
   a) who was appointed

b) is appointed
c) that is appointed

683. Choose the right answer: "It is only recently that ballets have been based on themes ... American life.".
   a) reflects
   b) is reflecting
   c) reflecting

684. Choose the right answer: "Cellulose, which ... for making paper, is found in all plants.".
   a) are used
   b) is using
   c) is used

685. Choose the right answer: "... children master the basics, advanced development becomes easier.".
   a) That
   b) Once
   c) Even

686. Choose the right answer: "The final examination was cancelled ...".
   a) although there was only one day to go
   b) only one day to go
   c) one day to go

687. Choose the right answer: "The chairman requested that ...".
   a) with more carefulness the problem could be studied
   b) the members study the problem more carefully
   c) the problem was more carefulnessly studied

688. Choose the right answer: "The saturated fat in dairy foods is thought ... a factor in heart disease.".
   a) as being
   b) to be
   c) it is

689. Choose the right answer: "... problems in sailing in tropical seas is the coral reefs.".
   a) There are the biggest

b) One of the biggest

c) Of the biggest one

690. Choose the right answer: "The bombardier beetle gets its name because ... its prey with caustic liquid.".

 a) it shoots

 b) shooting

 c) of it shoots

691. Choose the right answer: "... discussion would be complete without a consideration of national character.".

 a) None

 b) Not

 c) No

692. Choose the right answer: "She gave ...".

 a) the class a tough assignment

 b) to the class a tough assignments

 c) an assignment very tough

693. Choose the right answer: "... in the world export uranium.".

 a) Only little nations

 b) Only a few nations

 c) Only a little nation

694. Choose the right answer: "The lights and appliances in most homes use alternating current ...".

 a) instead of direct current

 b) for direct current instead

 c) that instead direct current

695. Choose the right answer: "Before penicillin was discovered, many people died ...".

 a) infected with simple bacteria

 b) infecting of simple bacteria

 c) from simple bacterial infections

696. Choose the right answer: "... they lost most of their lands to whites and were moved into other territories.".

 a) In spite of resistance

b) Spite resistance

c) Spite of resistance

697. Choose the right answer: "People who have very little technical background have ... to understand computer language.".
    a) learning
    b) learned
    c) learns

698. Choose the right answer: "It is recommendation of many psychologists ... to associate words and remember them.".
    a) mental images are used
    b) a learner to use mental images
    c) that a learner use mental images

699. Choose the right answer: "A bat will often spend the daylight hours ... upside down in a tree or a cave.".
    a) hanging
    b) that is
    c) hangs

700. Choose the right answer: "This man ... a submarine in 1825.".
    a) has built
    b) built
    c) he built

Set VIII

701. Choose the right answer: "The rhinoceros has a rather poor sense of smell, nor ...".
    a) well can it see
    b) it can see well
    c) can it see well

702. Choose the right answer: "Before ..., they used horse-drawn carts.".
    a) farmers had tractors
    b) having tractors farmers
    c) tractors owned by farmers

703. Choose the right answer: "... for overall health.".
    a) One's diet is helpful in extra fiber
    b) Extra fiber in one's diet is helpful
    c) Helpful one's diet is extra fiber

704. Choose the right answer: "Black, red and even other colors of diamonds ...".
    a) occasionally to find
    b) have occasionally been found
    c) occasionally found

705. Choose the right answer: "Had the fire been worse, the whole building ... to the ground.".
    a) will burn
    b) had burned
    c) would have burned

706. Choose the right answer: "The student was told that he could hand in the lost wallet to ...".
    a) anyone official
    b) official anyone
    c) officially anyone

707. Choose the right answer: "The changes in this city have occurred ...".
    a) with swifness
    b) in rapid ways
    c) rapidly

708. Choose the right answer: "She hasn't begun working on her Ph.D. ... working on her nuclear project.".
    a) yet as a result she is still
    b) yet because she is still
    c) still while she is already

709. Choose the right answer: "... actress's life is in many ways unlike that of other women.".
    a) An
    b) As the
    c) That the

710. Choose the right answer: "Management ... as the organization and coordination of an enterprise.".
    a) definable
    b) it is defined
    c) can be defined

711. Choose the right answer: "Beavers have been known to use logs and other natural resources to build dams that are more than a thousand ...".
    a) feet long
    b) long feet
    c) foot in length

712. Choose the right answer: "These university's programs ... those of Harvard.".
    a) come second after
    b) are second only to
    c) are first except for

713. Choose the right answer: "... created the donkey and elephant that symbolize the Democratic and Republican parties.".
    a) Thomas Nast, who
    b) It was Thomas Nast who
    c) Although Thomas Nast

714. Choose the right answer: "An equilateral triangle is a triangle ... and three angles of equal size.".
    a) that has three sides of equal length

b) it has three sides equally long

c) having three equal length sides in it

715. Choose the right answer: "The definition for "gram calories" is ... for most engineering work.".

    a) enough accurate

    b) accurate as enough

    c) accurate enough

716. Choose the right answer: "When your body does not get ..., it cannot make the glucose it needs.".

    a) enough food

    b) food as enough

    c) food enoughly

717. Choose the right answer: "She advocated teaching methods that provided teaching experiences for students to participate in ... material to memorize.".

    a) although

    b) instead of

    c) contrasting

718. Choose the right answer: "In a liberal arts curriculum, it is assumed that graduates will ... about languages, literature, history and other social sciences.".

    a) know how

    b) knowing

    c) know

719. Choose the right answer: "Please ... copies of copyrighted material without the permission of the publisher.".

    a) don't make

    b) not make

    c) not to make

720. Choose the right answer: "Not until a monkey is several years old ... to exhibit signs of independence.".

    a) and begin

    b) does it begin

    c) it begins

721. Choose the right answer: "... the plow is being displaced by new techniques that protect the land.".
    a) Wholly
    b) As a whole
    c) The whole

722. Choose the right answer: "Birds all over the world ... in distances up to thousands of kilometers.".
    a) migrating
    b) are migrated
    c) migrate

723. Choose the right answer: "... business, a merger is a combination of two or more companies.".
    a) In
    b) At
    c) The

724. Choose the right answer: "Studies indicate ... collecting art today than ever before.".
    a) more people that are
    b) that there are more people
    c) people are there

725. Choose the right answer: "The girl thought the fruit tasted ... and wanted to eat more.".
    a) sweet
    b) sweetly
    c) sweetened

726. Choose the right answer: "While attempting to reach his home before the hurricane, ...".
    a) the bicycle of Steve broke down
    b) the hurricane caught Steve
    c) Steve had an accident on his bicycle

727. Choose the right answer: "Unlike most Europeans, many Americans ... bacon and eggs for breakfast.".
    a) are used to eating

b) used to eat

c) used to eating

728. Choose the right answer: "Fire safety in family houses, ... most fire death occur, is difficult to achieve these years.".

   a) how
   b) where
   c) when

729. Choose the right answer: "... ants live in colonies, keep farms and have a society somewhat like human beings.".

   a) That is studied
   b) That the studies of ant life
   c) Studies of ant life show that

730. Choose the right answer: "... like "KFC" have used franchising to extend their sales.".

   a) Chain restaurants
   b) Chains restaurants
   c) Chains restaurant

731. Choose the right answer: "... have a powerful influence on the shape of the entire magazine industry.".

   a) That economical principle
   b) Economic principles
   c) Economic principles that

732. Choose the right answer: "... is cheaper for people who maintain a B average because they are a better risk than average people.".

   a) Automobile insurance
   b) Insurance of automobiles
   c) Insurance automobile

733. Choose the right answer: "... a mayor, many city governments employ a city manager.".

   a) And
   b) Also
   c) Besides

734. Choose the right answer: "If humans were totally deprived of sleep, they ... hallucinations and anxiety.".
    a) would experience
    b) experience
    c) had experienced

735. Choose the right answer: "In November of 1924, this city ...".
    a) completely burned it
    b) was completely burned
    c) it was burned completely

736. Choose the right answer: "... this city proximity to New York, it is an important link in the nation's transportation system.".
    a) However
    b) Resulting
    c) Because of

737. Choose the right answer: "The Federal Reserve System, ..., plays a key role in regulating the U.S. economy.".
    a) in 1913 they established it
    b) established in 1913
    c) was established in 1913

738. Choose the right answer: "... young, she traveled with her mother.".
    a) When she was
    b) Was she
    c) She was

739. Choose the right answer: "This strawberry was used in colonial times ...".
    a) bread was flavored
    b) flavored bread
    c) to flavor bread

740. Choose the right answer: "Touch-typing was originally devised as an aid to ...".
    a) the blind
    b) blinds
    c) a blind one

741. Choose the right answer: "When the president became very ill, his wife began to take a more active role in politics and many people believed that ... and the president shared some responsibilities.".
    a) her
    b) hers
    c) she

742. Choose the right answer: "In this country ... is the most concentrated is Boston.".
    a) the city where French influence
    b) French influence the city
    c) where the French influence the city

743. Choose the right answer: "... he was writings his plays and poems centuries ago, his ideas are still relevant today.".
    a) While
    b) Although
    c) When

744. Choose the right answer: "The wonders of the wild have inspired not only artists ...".
    a) but writers
    b) and also writers
    c) but writers too

745. Choose the right answer: "They are planning to build a subway, but it ... be a difficult undertaking.".
    a) can
    b) should
    c) might

746. Choose the right answer: "The people at the party were worried about her because no one was aware ... she had gone.".
    a) where that
    b) of where
    c) the place

747. Choose the right answer: "Green and magenta are complementary colors, ...".
    a) and blue and yellow so

b) and so blue and yellow do
c) and so are blue and yellow

748. Choose the right answer: "... that gold was discovered in this area.".
a) It was in 1848
b) In 1848 that it was
c) That in 1848

749. Choose the right answer: "Between this coast range and the Sierra Nevada ...".
a) lies the great Central Valley
b) being the great Central Valley
c) the great Central Valley

750. Choose the right answer: "Sunspots are known to cause ... enormous increase in radiation.".
a) one
b) some
c) an

751. Choose the right answer: "... the 25 years between the events, the population of this country doubled.".
a) Into
b) In
c) To

752. Choose the right answer: "In xerox printing, the ink becomes fused to the paper as soon as ...".
a) the paper heated
b) the paper is heated
c) heating the paper

753. Choose the right answer: "In the stringed instruments, the tones ... by playing a bow across a set of strings.".
a) are produced
b) they produce
c) producing

754. Choose the right answer: "After the purchase of this area, this country had ... it had previously owned.".

a) twice more lands than
b) two time much land than
c) twice as much land as

755. Choose the right answer: "Young rivers have no flood plains and their valleys are …".
a) narrowly
b) very narrow
c) narrowed

756. Choose the right answer: "… a bridge builder, Gustav Eiffel designed the Eiffel Tower.".
a) It while was
b) While
c) It was when

757. Choose the right answer: "In 2002 the President replaced Hasphire … of the new state.".
a) as the capital of
b) the capital being
c) the capital was

758. Choose the right answer: "Whole-grain food products … in large supermarkets across the country.".
a) now to purchase
b) the purchase of which
c) can now be purchased

759. Choose the right answer: "That year saw the first appearance of the movie, … the director created of character of Merlin.".
a) in it
b) in which
c) there

760. Choose the right answer: "Smith was most famous for his poetry, but … a schoolteacher and a musician.".
a) he was also
b) was including
c) moreover he

761. Choose the right answer: "... Java Man is the first manlike animal.".
	a) Believed generally is
	b) It is generally believed
	c) That it is generally believed

762. Choose the right answer: "Each mediocre book we read means one less great book that we would otherwise have a chance ...".
	a) to read them
	b) reading
	c) to read

763. Choose the right answer: "It is possible ... may assist some trees in saving water in the winter.".
	a) that the loss of leaves
	b) to lose leaves
	c) when leaves have lost

764. Choose the right answer: "Brian walked by the director's office ... would be in.".
	a) he will hope
	b) hoping he
	c) hoped

765. Choose the right answer: "The chairman arrived ... than all the other board members.".
	a) more early
	b) the earliest
	c) earlier

766. Choose the right answer: "The cockroach ... disease wherever it goes is regarded as a danger to public health.".
	a) spreading
	b) to spread
	c) which spreading

767. Choose the right answer: "This state relies heavily on income from crops, and ...".
	a) so does Japan
	b) Japan also
	c) Japan too

768. Choose the right answer: "… she began to make friends more easily.".
    a) Upon entering into the new school
    b) When she had been entering the new school
    c) After entering the new school

769. Choose the right answer: "Warmth, moisture and oxygen are requirements … most seeds.".
    a) can cultivate
    b) for cultivating
    c) for cultivate

770. Choose the right answer: "It costs about 40 euros to have a tooth …".
    a) filled
    b) to fill
    c) fill

771. Choose the right answer: "Due primarily to … the community broke up.".
    a) internal stresses of it
    b) internal stresses
    c) it had internal stresses

772. Choose the right answer: "The examiner made us … our identification number.".
    a) show
    b) to show
    c) showing

773. Choose the right answer: "Trapeze artists rely on safety nets … through the air.".
    a) they fly
    b) which fly
    c) when flying

774. Choose the right answer: "… have captured the spirit of the conquest of America as well as Cooper.".
    a) Few writers
    b) The few writers
    c) Few are the writers

775. Choose the right answer: "One purpose ... to decide if there is sufficient evidence.".
   a) of a grand jury
   b) of a grand jury is
   c) of a grand jury which is

776. Choose the right answer: "... jellies, jams are made by retaining the pulp.".
   a) Dislike
   b) Not alike
   c) Unlike

777. Choose the right answer: "Water, ... is also one of the most abundant compounds on earth.".
   a) one of the most critical elements for human survival
   b) of which one of the most critical elements for human survival
   c) is one of the most critical elements for human survival

778. Choose the right answer: "According to recent investigations, unselfish motives, such as empathy and ..., sometimes surpass self-interest.".
   a) to have solidarity with others
   b) solidarity with others
   c) one has solidarity with others

779. Choose the right answer: "The role of the mass media in influencing public policy decision and ... outlets for different types of views is enormous.".
   a) provide
   b) providing
   c) as it provides

780. Choose the right answer: "Public television stations are different from commercial stations ...".
   a) in areas of funding and programming
   b) for money and program types
   c) because they receive money differently and different type of shows

781. Choose the right answer: "Your behaviour makes me …".
- a) angrily
- b) in danger
- c) angry

782. Choose the right answer: "The price of the meal … a service charge.".
- a) includes
- b) enters
- c) encloses

783. Choose the right answer: "This … invention of yours should make you rich.".
- a) talented
- b) ingenious
- c) genial

784. Choose the right answer: "There were so … people in the queue for tickets that I missed the train.".
- a) few
- b) many
- c) much

785. Choose the right answer: "Many people think that Smith is a …-looking actor.".
- a) good
- b) better
- c) well

786. Choose the right answer: "Would you risk … $250 on a horse?".
- a) you bet
- b) betting
- c) to bet

787. Choose the right answer: "He always … over to my house after he had done his homework.".
- a) went
- b) gone
- c) came

788. Choose the right answer: "If ... it would stop raining for a morning, I could cut the grass.".
    a) just
    b) ever
    c) only

789. Choose the right answer: "A copy of our spring brochure is ... with this letter.".
    a) enclosed
    b) combined
    c) attached

790. Choose the right answer: "You thought I did wrong but the results ... my action.".
    a) agree
    b) justify
    c) prove

791. Choose the right answer: "Never ..., we'll see the movie next Friday.".
    a) to mind
    b) in mind
    c) you mind

792. Choose the right answer: "Some schools have ... rules of behaviour which must be obeyed.".
    a) strict
    b) solid
    c) strong

793. Choose the right answer: "I was told that ... I gave up smoking my illness would get much worse.".
    a) without
    b) unless
    c) except

794. Choose the right answer: "Our car was ... in the accident.".
    a) harmed
    b) hurt
    c) damaged

795. Choose the right answer: "It took our economies many years to ... from the oil crisis.".
    a) recover
    b) regain
    c) retain

796. Choose the right answer: "It doesn't sound ... he knows anything about it.".
    a) so as
    b) as if
    c) that is

797. Choose the right answer: "Without money you will be ... to do anything.".
    a) powerful
    b) overpowered
    c) powerless

798. Choose the right answer: "He delights ... annoying me.".
    a) in
    b) with
    c) at

799. Choose the right answer: "They would find another hotel if their rooms ... for them.".
    a) won't be prepared
    b) weren't prepared
    c) aren't prepared

800. Choose the right answer: "I'm not surprised they are in a mess. It's not exactly ...-shattering news.".
    a) spinner
    b) till
    c) earth

Set IX

801. Choose the right answer: "On the first morning I woke up covered in mosquito ...".
    a) bites
    b) pricks
    c) stings

802. Choose the right answer: "Pointing ... people is rude!".
    a) out
    b) at
    c) on

803. Choose the right answer: "Mr. Smith ... the company in the way he wanted to.".
    a) ruled
    b) commanded
    c) ran

804. Choose the right answer: "He ... the headwaiter about the slow service.".
    a) questioned
    b) argued
    c) disputed

805. Choose the right answer: "My cousin is much better than I am ... football.".
    a) for playing
    b) at playing
    c) to play

806. Choose the right answer: "The purpose of the examination was to ... the students' knowledge of the subject.".
    a) test
    b) try
    c) prove

807. Choose the right answer: "From my point of view, it wasn't a very good ...".
    a) deal

b) dealt
c) exchanged

808. Choose the right answer: "I wish you ... make such a noise.".
a) wouldn't
b) shouldn't
c) needn't

809. Choose the right answer: "I think you ought to talk to Steven; he's got ... interesting information.".
a) any
b) a
c) some

810. Choose the right answer: "My cousin is a parachute ...".
a) teacher
b) instructor
c) educator

811. Choose the right answer: "In her ... she was a famous table tennis player.".
a) day
b) year
c) hour

812. Choose the right answer: "She wasn't' keen ... going to stay with her aunt.".
a) for
b) on
c) of

813. Choose the right answer: "Sarah came home from work ... very tired and depressed.".
a) to look
b) looked
c) looking

814. Choose the right answer: "We haven't ... thought of going abroad for a holiday.".
a) ever

b) always
c) yet

815. Choose the right answer: "... each school year all the children were given copies of behaviour rules.".
    a) To start with
    b) At the beginning of
    c) At first

816. Choose the right answer: "You shouldn't persist ... bothering her.".
    a) with
    b) to
    c) in

817. Choose the right answer: "She ... spends her holidays in the mountains because she loves fresh air.".
    a) rarely
    b) usually
    c) invariably

818. Choose the right answer: "By half past twelve tomorrow I ... along the motorway.".
    a) will be driving
    b) will drive
    c) drive

819. Choose the right answer: "Conversations you strike up with travel mates usually tend to be ...".
    a) perverse
    b) trivial
    c) imperative

820. Choose the right answer: "The Boston coach ... at 09:30 a.m.".
    a) reaches
    b) travels
    c) leaves

821. Choose the right answer: "You only master a skill by ... it a lot.".
    a) doing

b) practicing
c) doing

822. Choose the right answer: "I'm afraid a rise in salary is ... just now.".
a) out of the question
b) out of date
c) out of sight

823. Choose the right answer: "I'll ... the children for you.".
a) look out
b) look for
c) look after

824. Choose the right answer: "They ... to get married in that church.".
a) selected
b) judged
c) decided

825. Choose the right answer: "Have you a rough ... of how many people are coming to the party?".
a) idea
b) hope
c) imagination

826. Choose the right answer: "As the waiter crossed the restaurant, he ... over someone's foot.".
a) swept
b) tripped
c) knocked

827. Choose the right answer: "When she heard the terrible noise she asked me what was ... on.".
a) being
b) getting
c) going

828. Choose the right answer: "I don't think that blue dress ... her.".
a) suits
b) cheers
c) agrees

829. Choose the right answer: "She … a very interesting story.".
	a) talked
	b) spoke
	c) told

830. Choose the right answer: "In pain as a result of the fall, the man … slowly home.".
	a) limped
	b) sped
	c) wound

831. Choose the right answer: "Three … beers, please.".
	a) chilled
	b) icy
	c) frozen

832. Choose the right answer: "Blood-… are urgently required.".
	a) bankers
	b) donors
	c) suckers

833. Choose the right answer: "The child was so poor that she had to wander the streets and … for money.".
	a) demand
	b) appeal
	c) beg

834. Choose the right answer: "I don't agree … you.".
	a) at
	b) with
	c) on

835. Choose the right answer: "Sarah is accustomed … living in comfort.".
	a) to
	b) with
	c) at

836. Choose the right answer: "I drew a lot of money … the bank yesterday.".
	a) in

b) on

c) from

837. Choose the right answer: "I wouldn't have been ill if I ... on that trip.".
    a) don't go
    b) hadn't gone
    c) haven't gone

838. Choose the right answer: "The doctor arranged for me to see the ... at the hospital.".
    a) specialist
    b) expertise
    c) expert

839. Choose the right answer: "I'm angry with the way I've been treated by this firm. I've had it up to ... with the way I've been treated.".
    a) roof
    b) spare
    c) here

840. Choose the right answer: "I was somewhat suspicious ... her over-confident manner.".
    a) by
    b) of
    c) with

841. Choose the right answer: "I was afraid of losing my suitcase so I tied a ... on it.".
    a) mark
    b) label
    c) notice

842. Choose the right answer: "I am not sure, but ... I know she has decided to accept the job.".
    a) as far as
    b) as long as
    c) according

843. Choose the right answer: "Brian is such a perfectionist that it's ...".
    a) sleepy

b) fatigued
c) exhausting

844. Choose the right answer: "You must ... that your safety belt is fastened.".
    a) secure
    b) check
    c) guarantee

845. Choose the right answer: "..., after trying multiple times, he passed the examination.".
    a) At last
    b) Last
    c) Last of all

846. Choose the right answer: "That was no accident: you did it on ...!".
    a) plan
    b) intention
    c) purpose

847. Choose the right answer: "I was just ... to go out when you called.".
    a) planned
    b) about
    c) around

848. Choose the right answer: "The witness told the court that he ... the accused before.".
    a) didn't see
    b) hasn't seen
    c) had never seen

849. Choose the right answer: "In order to ... with her studies she worked through the summer.".
    a) catch up
    b) take on
    c) take up

850. Choose the right answer: "The tea is very hot; you'll have to ... it.".
    a) sip

b) gulp
c) swallow

851. Choose the right answer: "This car is in terrible condition. You … have an accident at any time.".
a) should
b) could
c) can

852. Choose the right answer: "I think you'd better … and see me next week.".
a) came
b) come
c) to come

853. Choose the right answer: "He may be quick at understanding, but he is not capable … remembering anything.".
a) to
b) of
c) in

854. Choose the right answer: "She was found guilty … murder and condemned to death.".
a) of
b) for
c) with

855. Choose the right answer: "She is indifferent … other people.".
a) at
b) of
c) to

856. Choose the right answer: "… at the party!".
a) Have fun
b) Make fun
c) Do fun

857. Choose the right answer: "All people experience good as well as bad things …".
a) in lifetime

b) in life
c) in lives

858. Choose the right answer: "I can't remember when all those books …".
	a) are being bought
	b) had been bought
	c) have been bought

859. Choose the right answer: "If we went there, we … some of the museums.".
	a) would visit
	b) visited
	c) will visit

860. Choose the right answer: "I find it difficult sometimes to … between purple and blue.".
	a) classify
	b) discriminate
	c) categorize

861. Choose the right answer: "The new factory must be finished … as the profitability of the organization depends on it.".
	a) on time
	b) at time
	c) for a time

862. Choose the right answer: "The colour of the handle does not … so long as it is the right size.".
	a) worry
	b) concern
	c) matter

863. Choose the right answer: "We went to the railway station to … our friends …".
	a) tell/goodbye
	b) see/off
	c) set/out

864. Choose the right answer: "She shouldn't be allowed to play in the club. She's not a …".

a) partner
b) member
c) belong

865. Choose the right answer: "After a day of housework I am totally …".
a) exhausted
b) weak
c) strained

866. Choose the right answer: "There is no reason to … his honesty.".
a) ask
b) search
c) doubt

867. Choose the right answer: "The constant … on their hands causes injury.".
a) grip
b) movement
c) pressure

868. Choose the right answer: "The League of Nations was set … after the First World War.".
a) up
b) off
c) down

869. Choose the right answer: "All good things must come to … end.".
a) one
b) an
c) the

870. Choose the right answer: "The performance had to be cancelled … of the illness of the leading actress.".
a) because
b) due
c) according

871. Choose the right answer: "Buses and metros are the most important forms of public … in this city.".
a) travel

b) traffic
c) transport

872. Choose the right answer: "You should have told me you were married, ...?".
a) isn't it
b) shouldn't you
c) didn't you

873. Choose the right answer: "The books I borrowed are overdue. I'll take them back to the ...".
a) bible
b) magazine
c) library

874. Choose the right answer: "The actor enjoys giving ... of poems.".
a) recitations
b) repetitions
c) rehearsals

875. Choose the right answer: "The phone is ringing. Could you ... please?".
a) hand it down
b) pick it up
c) take it up

876. Choose the right answer: "With one engine of the plane out of action, it had been ... over the Channel.".
a) fly and sit
b) start and return
c) touch and go

877. Choose the right answer: "All the travel arrangements ... before we received a letter from her.".
a) had been made
b) were being made
c) are being made

878. Choose the right answer: "The last meeting of our section ... on 15th November.".

a) held
b) was held
c) has been held

879. Choose the right answer: "You are still working on your essay. I think you ... it by four o'clock.".
a) should have finished
b) have been finishing
c) must have finished

880. Choose the right answer: "sharp practices = ...".
a) aggressive marketing
b) unprofitable business
c) dishonest methods in business

881. Choose the right answer: "It is usually better not to ... things, in case they are not returned.".
a) offer
b) lend
c) borrow

882. Choose the right answer: "It's five years now since the Socialists came to ... in this country.".
a) power
b) force
c) control

883. Choose the right answer: "She was killed in a car ...".
a) blow
b) hit
c) crash

884. Choose the right answer: "It's nearly one year since I last ... to a dentist.".
a) went
b) had gone
c) been going

885. Choose the right answer: "The civil servant ... his post because he disagreed with the director.".

a) gave in
b) gave up
c) gave off

886. Choose the right answer: "I don't know where she lives now; she left this area many years …".
a) before
b) away
c) ago

887. Choose the right answer: "There was a sudden loud … which made everyone jump.".
a) split
b) stroke
c) bang

888. Choose the right answer: "The bill came to over a thousand euros …".
a) in all
b) to all
c) of all

889. Choose the right answer: "Her remarks on television about the strike … the Prime Minister so much that she was sacked.".
a) disliked
b) displeased
c) disordered

890. Choose the right answer: "The police have issued a full … of the murderer.".
a) notice
b) detail
c) description

891. Choose the right answer: "A lot of people find … art very difficult to understand.".
a) contemporary
b) actual
c) current

892. Choose the right answer: "He was ... of understanding anything that involved numbers.".
   a) unable
   b) useless
   c) incapable

893. Choose the right answer: "If there's ... for complaint, please inform the manager.".
   a) fear
   b) cause
   c) opportunity

894. Choose the right answer: "There was ... enough cake for all of us to have a small slice.".
   a) just
   b) really
   c) around

895. Choose the right answer: "She was bitten by a mosquito, but she made things worse by ... the bite.".
   a) stroking
   b) rubbing
   c) scratching

896. Choose the right answer: "Contrary ... my expectations there was no need to be uneasy about the final results.".
   a) from
   b) for
   c) to

897. Choose the right answer: "She prides herself ... her clean house.".
   a) on
   b) with
   c) in

898. Choose the right answer: "Your conclusions are not consistent ... the facts.".
   a) against
   b) with
   c) to

899. Choose the right answer: "The coin was too small ... in the grass.".
   a) as for Steve see it
   b) for Steve not see it
   c) for Steve to see it

900. Choose the right answer: "This book ... in Europe for more than twenty days by now.".
   a) has been published
   b) is published
   c) was published

Set X

901. Choose the right answer: "Pioneer men and women endured hardships and ...".
    a) also the childs
    b) so did their children
    c) so do their children

902. Choose the right answer: "The rains of 2020 ... the river to overflow resulted in one of the worst floods of this century.".
    a) caused
    b) causing
    c) they caused

903. Choose the right answer: "The CPI lists ...".
    a) how much costs every car
    b) how much does every car cost
    c) how much every car costs

904. Choose the right answer: "Professional people appreciate ... when it is necessary to cancel an appointment.".
    a) your calling them
    b) you to call them
    c) that you are calling them

905. Choose the right answer: "A student should tell a dorm counselor if ... live with his roommate again next year.".
    a) he'll rather not
    b) he'd rather not
    c) he won't rather

906. Choose the right answer: "It's the first time that the Princess has been to Russia, ...?".
    a) isn't it
    b) hasn't it
    c) hasn't she

907. Choose the right answer: "He is considered by most art critics ... greatest portrait painter.".
    a) who was the

b) that he was
c) the

908. Choose the right answer: "They brought the popular custom of Halloween to America ... 1840s.".
a) during
b) in the
c) within

909. Choose the right answer: "... that increasing numbers of laptops will be bought.".
a) It is anticipated
b) Anticipating
c) In anticipation

910. Choose the right answer: "The volume of this valley is fifty times ... National Valley.".
a) than of
b) that of
c) of

911. Choose the right answer: "... categorized as lipids.".
a) Fats and also oils
b) Fats and oils
c) Fats and oils are

912. Choose the right answer: "Benny would have studied medicine if he ... to a medical school.".
a) was admitted
b) had been admitted
c) could be able to enter

913. Choose the right answer: "The jurors were told to ...".
a) talk all they wanted
b) speak freely
c) make lots of expressions

914. Choose the right answer: "We had hoped ... the game, but the other team played very well.".
a) that our team would win

b) that our team win

c) our team to win

915. Choose the right answer: "The postal service policy for check approval includes a requirement that two pieces of identification …".
    a) be presented
    b) must present
    c) for presentation

916. Choose the right answer: "In order for people who spoke different languages to engage in trade …, they developed a simplified language.".
    a) with each the other
    b) with each another
    c) with each other

917. Choose the right answer: "The Supreme Court doesn't hear a case unless …".
    a) already tried
    b) it already trying
    c) it has already been tried

918. Choose the right answer: "Experience has shown that even well-trained … success in forecasting interest rates.".
    a) experts do not always have
    b) do not always have experts
    c) always do not have experts

919. Choose the right answer: "The financial manager's job … among the sources of finance.".
    a) to shop around is
    b) is to shop around
    c) is it to shop around

920. Choose the right answer: "This Council is said … from 1459.".
    a) to date
    b) dating
    c) it dates

921. Choose the right answer: "When Brian arrived home after a hard day at work, …".

a) his wife slept
b) his wife was sleeping
c) his wife has been sleeping

922. Choose the right answer: "Kitchen appliances called blenders became ... in the 1950s.".
a) establishing
b) which establish
c) established

923. Choose the right answer: "Sometimes ... wears people out and is worse than the lack of sleep itself.".
a) the desire to sleep
b) to desire sleep is
c) the desire to sleep who

924. Choose the right answer: "Adrian said that no other car could go ...".
a) so fast like his car
b) as fast like his car
c) as fast as his car

925. Choose the right answer: "The attorney told his client that ...".
a) the case had a minimum chance to be won by they
b) they had little chance of winning the case
c) it was nearly impossible to win him the case

926. Choose the right answer: "Doctoral students have been studying in the library every night ... the last three months.".
a) for
b) before
c) since

927. Choose the right answer: "The IRS ... their tax forms by April 15.".
a) make all Americans filing
b) makes all Americans to file
c) makes all Americans file

928. Choose the right answer: "... pitched his first major-league game, Daniel was only fourteen years old.".
a) When he

b) Because of he

c) He

929. Choose the right answer: "... occasions for congratulations.".
    a) That considered birthdays usually
    b) Birthdays are usually considered
    c) Usually considering birthdays

930. Choose the right answer: "..., he would have signed his name in the corner.".
    a) If he paints that picture
    b) If he painted that picture
    c) If he had painted that picture

931. Choose the right answer: "At certain times of the year, smog in the Arctic is thicker ... anywhere else on earth.".
    a) of smog
    b) than smog
    c) smog

932. Choose the right answer: "The speaker is ...".
    a) a person who has close awareness
    b) very well acquainted with the subject
    c) someone who knows well enough about the subject undertaken to do the speaking

933. Choose the right answer: "Rocks are formed below the surface of the earth ... high temperatures and pressures.".
    a) there are
    b) there are where
    c) where there are

934. Choose the right answer: "In his inaugural speech, the manager ... that we should not ask anything about his past.".
    a) said
    b) did
    c) told

935. Choose the right answer: "There are three kids of solar eclipses: one is total, another is annular and ...".

a) the other is partial
b) other is partial
c) the another is partial

936. Choose the right answer: "Keynes argued that to avoid an economic depression the government ... spending and lower interest rates.".
a) higher
b) should increase
c) is

937. Choose the right answer: "A hero of the war, ... President of the country.".
a) he later became
b) that he later became
c) later became he

938. Choose the right answer: "The various types of bacteria are classified according to ... shaped.".
a) whose
b) they have
c) how they are

939. Choose the right answer: "Franchising offers many advantages to business owners ... problematic.".
a) it is
b) even though it is
c) despite its

940. Choose the right answer: "Sarah changed her major from French to business ...".
a) hoping to find a job more easily
b) with hopes to be able easier to locate employment
c) hoping she can easier get a job

941. Choose the right answer: "Equipment would have to be capable of drilling through 100,000 feet of rock to investigate the mantle ...".
a) beneath their
b) beneath its
c) beneath them

942. Choose the right answer: "Drivers should look very carefully ... onto the main street.".
   a) turn
   b) they turn
   c) when turning

943. Choose the right answer: "She taught ... to play the guitar.".
   a) hers
   b) herself
   c) his

944. Choose the right answer: "The people of this area have been considering ... themselves from the rest of the provinces.".
   a) to separate
   b) separate
   c) separating

945. Choose the right answer: "The greater the demand, ... the price.".
   a) the higher
   b) higher
   c) the high

946. Choose the right answer: "Many plants can grow in water ... nutrients are added.".
   a) above all
   b) as long as
   c) sure that

947. Choose the right answer: "The teacher suggested that her students ... summer experiences.".
   a) write a composition on their
   b) had written any compositions for his
   c) wrote some compositions of his or her

948. Choose the right answer: "It was not until she arrived in class ... realized she had forgotten her book.".
   a) when she
   b) that she
   c) she

949. Choose the right answer: "This territory, an area … the size of Paris, was bought last year.".
    a) is four times more than
    b) four times than more
    c) more than four times

950. Choose the right answer: "Magellan never completed the first circumnavigation of the world and …".
    a) neither did most of his crew
    b) and most of his crew didn't too
    c) and most of his crew didn't also

951. Choose the right answer: "… "cultural diffusion" refers to the spread of customs from one culture to another.".
    a) To phrase
    b) The phrase
    c) To the phrase

952. Choose the right answer: "Amniocentesis can be used not only to diagnose fetal disorder … the sex of the child.".
    a) but determining
    b) but to determine
    c) but also to determine

953. Choose the right answer: "The adder is a venomous snake … bite may be fatal.".
    a) whose
    b) its
    c) that

954. Choose the right answer: "… of the Stamp Act provoked strong opposition.".
    a) Before the passage
    b) The passage
    c) The passage was

955. Choose the right answer: "An elephant can lift … a ton with its tusks.".
    a) as much as
    b) them
    c) most

956. Choose the right answer: "The human brain ... only two percent of the body weight.".
- a) makes it up
- b) which makes up
- c) makes up

957. Choose the right answer: "Scientists are not sure ...".
- a) can cold fusion occur
- b) precisely how could fusion can occur
- c) how precisely can cold fusion occur

958. Choose the right answer: "In the 1970s, pop art ... to discover new trends.".
- a) sought
- b) seeking
- c) has sought

959. Choose the right answer: "Nestled along the shoreline of the bay ...".
- a) near several recently settle Inuit communities
- b) are several recently settled Inuit communities
- c) is where several recently settled Inuit communities

960. Choose the right answer: "Glass that has been tempered may be up to ...".
- a) ordinary glass as hard as five times
- b) as hard as ordinary glass five times
- c) five times as hard as ordinary glass

961. Choose the right answer: "If more than seven thousand euros are transported into the country, a report needs ... with the customs office.".
- a) to be filed
- b) file
- c) to file

962. Choose the right answer: "Of the many novels, this is perhaps ... to many readers.".
- a) the more satisfying than
- b) the most satisfying one
- c) most satisfying one

963. Choose the right answer: "Rarely ... to the movie because he prefers to play computer games.".
    a) does Daniel go
    b) Daniel goes
    c) Daniel does go

964. Choose the right answer: "Speaking a foreign language is the best way to learn ...".
    a) it
    b) ours
    c) us

965. Choose the right answer: "Her grades have improved, but only ...".
    a) some
    b) minimum
    c) very slightly

966. Choose the right answer: "All the cereal grains ... grow on the prairies and plains of the country.".
    a) except the rice
    b) but rice
    c) excepting rice

967. Choose the right answer: "... the bones of prehistoric man, scientists hope to determine what they ate.".
    a) By studying
    b) In study of
    c) Studying

968. Choose the right answer: "..., she is also well known for her multivolume biographies.".
    a) An eminent American poet
    b) She is an eminent American poet
    c) Despite an eminent American poet

969. Choose the right answer: "Modern industrial methods have supplanted individual crafts, ..., stone carvers and cobblers extinct.".
    a) make blacksmiths
    b) making them blacksmiths
    c) making blacksmiths

970. Choose the right answer: "Lobbyists who represent special interest groups get ... that benefits their groups.".
   a) the legislation to pass by Congress
   b) Congress to pass the legislation
   c) Congress passed the legislation

971. Choose the right answer: "Weather makers can encourage two clouds to merge into one big cloud ... produce a thunderstorm.".
   a) and
   b) which
   c) these

972. Choose the right answer: "It is usually ... lava but gas that kills people during volcanic eruptions.".
   a) no
   b) neither
   c) not

973. Choose the right answer: "The Disney park in Japan is ... Paris or Florida.".
   a) larger the ones in
   b) larger than the ones in
   c) the largest of then ones

974. Choose the right answer: "... capital is the largest city in the state.".
   a) Is the
   b) The
   c) It is the

975. Choose the right answer: "Anthropologists ... within their environments and evaluate them.".
   a) study societies
   b) their societies are studied
   c) who study societies are

976. Choose the right answer: "People have used vast amounts of wood for building and ... their homes.".
   a) heat
   b) to heat
   c) heating

977. Choose the right answer: "... of the US grown during a Republican administration.".
    a) Rarely has the federal government
    b) Has the federal government rarely
    c) Rarely the federal government

978. Choose the right answer: "Overexposure to the sun can produce ... can some toxic chemicals.".
    a) more than damage to the skin
    b) more damage to the skin than
    c) damage more than to the skin

979. Choose the right answer: "Balinese cats ... medium length silky coats of fur.".
    a) which have
    b) they have
    c) have

980. Choose the right answer: "If one is suffering from a psychosomatic illness, one may feel very ...".
    a) worse
    b) bad
    c) badly

981. Choose the right answer: "... did he realize that there was danger.".
    a) Only after entering the store
    b) After he had entered the store
    c) Upon entering the store

982. Choose the right answer: "In mathematics, a variable is a symbol ... some element of a set.".
    a) represents that
    b) that represents
    c) represents

983. Choose the right answer: "Few natural elements exist in ... that they are rarely seen.".
    a) so small quantities
    b) small quantity
    c) such small quantities

984. Choose the right answer: "The janitor refused to unlock the door because he ... busy.".
   a) too
   b) was
   c) himself

985. Choose the right answer: "..., which is the highest in the range, appears very challenging.".
   a) Climbing the mountain
   b) The mountains
   c) Up the mountain

986. Choose the right answer: "The student managed to pass the entrance examination ... he was blind.".
   a) unless
   b) in spite of the fact
   c) because

987. Choose the right answer: "John Kennedy was ... to be assassinated.".
   a) the four
   b) four
   c) the fourth

988. Choose the right answer: "... the formulation of explanatory laws, the first step in scientific research is the collection of facts.".
   a) Although science's ultimate aim is
   b) Although it is science's ultimate aim
   c) Although science's ultimate being aim

989. Choose the right answer: "It is earth's gravity that ... people their weight.".
   a) give
   b) giving
   c) gives

990. Choose the right answer: "... that new information to anyone else but the sergeant.".
   a) They asked him to don't give
   b) They asked him not to give
   c) They asked him to no give

991. Choose the right answer: "Considered unique and exotic, …".
    a) the llama is kept as a pet in many households
    b) there are many households that keeps llamas as a pet
    c) the llama kept as a pet in many household

992. Choose the right answer: "The oldest theories of business cycles are … that linked their cause to fluctuations of the harvest.".
    a) them
    b) whatever
    c) those

993. Choose the right answer: "One of the few plants that can move about, … a wavy, gliding motion.".
    a) has
    b) having
    c) being

994. Choose the right answer: "The works of Picasso were quite … during various periods.".
    a) different than
    b) different
    c) differ

995. Choose the right answer: "The more hemoglobin one has, the more oxygen is carried to … cells.".
    a) one's
    b) its
    c) their

996. Choose the right answer: "… can be grown on arid land.".
    a) Only a little crops
    b) Only little crop
    c) Only a few crops

997. Choose the right answer: "… air traffic controllers guide planes through conditions of near zero visibility.".
    a) Talking with pilots and watching their approach on radar
    b) Talk with pilots and watch their approach on radar
    c) They talk with pilots and watch their approach on radar

998. Choose the right answer: "Culture influences the way ...".
- a) viewing the world
- b) that we view the world
- c) the world view

999. Choose the right answer: "Overexposure to the sun causes ... health problems.".
- a) various
- b) but
- c) among

1000. Choose the right answer: "The doctor told his receptionist that he would return ...".
- a) as early as it would be possible
- b) at the nearest early possibility
- c) as soon as possible

Set XI

1001. Choose the right answer: "I couldn't do question 4, so I ... it out.".
    a) left
    b) let
    c) put

1002. Choose the right answer: "I don't want to wait until tomorrow; I ... go at once.".
    a) want
    b) would rather
    c) prefer

1003. Choose the right answer: "The old man was very fond ... telling stories.".
    a) of
    b) for
    c) to

1004. Choose the right answer: "I am tired ... grammar exercises.".
    a) by do
    b) to do
    c) of doing

1005. Choose the right answer: "I am ... this essay right now.".
    a) finish
    b) to finish
    c) finished

1006. Choose the right answer: "Don't let him ... it.".
    a) doing
    b) to do
    c) do

1007. Choose the right answer: "How long ... English?".
    a) have you studied
    b) do you study
    c) did you studied

1008. Choose the right answer: "The doctor insists ... for a few days.".
- a) his resting
- b) that he rest
- c) that he is resting

1009. Choose the right answer: "You ... your seats today.".
- a) had to reserve better
- b) had better reserve
- c) had to better reserve

1010. Choose the right answer: "After he had researched and ... his paper, he found some errors.".
- a) written
- b) wrote
- c) writing

1011. Choose the right answer: "The new champion, ..., took over the dining room.".
- a) led by an equestrian
- b) accompanied by his entourage
- c) accompanied by his reveries

1012. Choose the right answer: "The three friends all ... for the same job.".
- a) applied
- b) referred
- c) requested

1013. Choose the right answer: "I knew him ... I was child.".
- a) until
- b) during
- c) when

1014. Choose the right answer: "The officer's orders were perfectly ...".
- a) applied
- b) executed
- c) developed

1015. Choose the right answer: "The manager has just gone on his ... leave.".
- a) annual

b) regular
c) permanent

1016. Choose the right answer: "Before the invention of refrigeration, the ... of fish and meat was a problem.".
    a) keeping
    b) treatment
    c) preservation

1017. Choose the right answer: "My brother did not go to school yesterday. Neither ...".
    a) went I
    b) did I
    c) had I gone

1018. Choose the right answer: "He ... for a job for some weeks.".
    a) has been looking
    b) has looked
    c) looks

1019. Choose the right answer: "The firm went bankrupt and their shares became ...".
    a) invaluable
    b) unworthy
    c) worthless

1020. Choose the right answer: "The ascent of this mountain is ... but anyone who makes it to the top is rewarded by a spectacular view.".
    a) unpleasant
    b) easy
    c) unique

1021. Choose the right answer: "When the soldiers were on the march, there was one man who was always out of ... with the rest.".
    a) step
    b) union
    c) times

1022. Choose the right answer: "It is not ... for you to eat too much.".
    a) well

b) good
c) useful

1023. Choose the right answer: "Can this be the little cat ... hair I used to stroke?".
   a) which
   b) who's
   c) whose

1024. Choose the right answer: "The reason I left is ... I was bored.".
   a) that
   b) why
   c) for

1025. Choose the right answer: "You're ... who noticed that.".
   a) the single
   b) the only one
   c) the only

1026. Choose the right answer: "We heard her ... to her little cousin.".
   a) talk
   b) talks
   c) talked

1027. Choose the right answer: "The team really looks because the coach had them ... every night this week.".
   a) the practise
   b) practised
   c) practise

1028. Choose the right answer: "Almost everyone fails ... the driver's test on the first try.".
   a) passing
   b) to pass
   c) in passing

1029. Choose the right answer: "She always asks my sister and ... for advice.".
   a) me

b) mine
c) I

1030. Choose the right answer: "I made a big mistake but nobody noticed and I got ... it.".
a) with
b) away with
c) towards

1031. Choose the right answer: "I'd be careful in my dealings with him. I'm sure he's up to no ...".
a) pretences
b) eel
c) good

1032. Choose the right answer: "Smith was an interesting man but sometimes he was a bit economical with the ...".
a) cock
b) truth
c) teeth

1033. Choose the right answer: "Try not to be too impatient ... him.".
a) with
b) at
c) for

1034. Choose the right answer: "I will succeed with ... help from my friends.".
a) a few
b) a little
c) few

1035. Choose the right answer: "The ... response I got from them drove me crazy.".
a) little
b) few
c) a few

1036. Choose the right answer: "Some authors are too ... to criticism.".
a) sensational

b) senseless

c) sensitive

1037. Choose the right answer: "After a lot of difficulties, he ... to open the door.".
- a) obtained
- b) realized
- c) managed

1038. Choose the right answer: "Do you want to wait? Four weeks ... too long for me to wait.".
- a) is
- b) were
- c) was

1039. Choose the right answer: "He did four hours' ... studying a day for the final exam.".
- a) big
- b) solid
- c) strong

1040. Choose the right answer: "... terrible weather!".
- a) What
- b) How
- c) How a

1041. Choose the right answer: "Daniel works from seven ... four.".
- a) in
- b) out
- c) to

1042. Choose the right answer: "Tell him ... some envelopes, please.".
- a) buy
- b) to buy
- c) buy to

1043. Choose the right answer: "We are a little late – the play ... begun.".
- a) has just
- b) is just
- c) just

1044. Choose the right answer: "I couldn't understand what they were ...".
    a) speaking
    b) saying
    c) talking

1045. Choose the right answer: "I don't like iced tea and ...".
    a) neither does she
    b) she doesn't neither
    c) either isn't she

1046. Choose the right answer: "Please ... photocopies of documents.".
    a) no submit
    b) not to submit
    c) do not submit

1047. Choose the right answer: "If I ... the flu I would have gone with you.".
    a) didn't have
    b) hadn't had
    c) wouldn't have had

1048. Choose the right answer: "We are looking forward ... you.".
    a) of seeing
    b) to seeing
    c) for seeing

1049. Choose the right answer: "It is imperative that you ... there in person.".
    a) be
    b) will be
    c) are

1050. Choose the right answer: "Something must be done quickly if endangered species ... saved.".
    a) can be
    b) be
    c) are to be

1051. Choose the right answer: "I would like to offer a small ... to any one who finds my missing cat.".

a) reward
b) expense
c) receipt

1052. Choose the right answer: "It was a big disappointment but I got ... it.".
    a) in
    b) over
    c) to

1053. Choose the right answer: "I've got a lot of work to get ... before I can go on holiday this year.".
    a) with
    b) in
    c) through

1054. Choose the right answer: "... for no help from anyone.".
    a) I asked
    b) I ain't asking
    c) I'm not requesting aid

1055. Choose the right answer: "Very few books published each year ... toward improving health.".
    a) make a significant contribution
    b) have a bad effect
    c) do a great deal of damage

1056. Choose the right answer: "The lady was moved to tears ... sorrow.".
    a) of
    b) with
    c) to

1057. Choose the right answer: "I was told that ... care could have prevented the accident.".
    a) few
    b) a few
    c) a little

1058. Choose the right answer: "I wanted some coffee but there was ... in the pot.".

a) nothing
b) none
c) no

1059. Choose the right answer: "He will take us to the town … we can see old temples.".
   a) where
   b) at it
   c) which

1060. Choose the right answer: "My dog … twice a day.".
   a) has eaten
   b) eats
   c) have eaten

1061. Choose the right answer: "She thanked … so kind.".
   a) us to be
   b) us for being
   c) that we were

1062. Choose the right answer: "I forgot to … her to buy some coffee.".
   a) repeat
   b) remember
   c) remind

1063. Choose the right answer: "I read an interesting … in a newspaper about farming today.".
   a) description
   b) article
   c) composition

1064. Choose the right answer: "We all … them good luck when they decided to emigrate.".
   a) wished
   b) told
   c) gave

1065. Choose the right answer: "They seem to get … very well together.".
   a) in

b) on

c) off

1066. Choose the right answer: "Some prisoners ... from their guards and escaped.".
   a) broke up
   b) broke out
   c) broke away

1067. Choose the right answer: "The students ... their classes about ten o'clock.".
   a) started
   b) have started
   c) had started

1068. Choose the right answer: "A cold wind ... for the last two days.".
   a) blew
   b) has been blowing
   c) blows

1069. Choose the right answer: "I ... this letter around for weeks.".
   a) am carrying
   b) was carrying
   c) have been carrying

1070. Choose the right answer: "The concert premiere was attended by ...".
   a) hundreds of music lovers
   b) large amounts of persons
   c) a vast horde of devotees

1071. Choose the right answer: "He ... being given a receipt.".
   a) asked to
   b) insisted on
   c) required

1072. Choose the right answer: "The secretary told me to ... on as he was talking to someone else.".
   a) hold

b) wait

c) carry

1073. Choose the right answer: "All of a ... there was an explosion and the lights went out.".
- a) time
- b) once
- c) sudden

1074. Choose the right answer: "Good parents should ... for their children.".
- a) supply
- b) provide
- c) support

1075. Choose the right answer: "When the flat is not occupied, it is ...".
- a) rented
- b) valueless
- c) vacant

1076. Choose the right answer: "I ... swim in this river when I was young.".
- a) used to
- b) use to
- c) am used to

1077. Choose the right answer: "My father got home ... ago.".
- a) a half hour
- b) half an hour
- c) a half an hour

1078. Choose the right answer: "Give the message to ... is at the desk!".
- a) whomever
- b) what
- c) whoever

1079. Choose the right answer: "In a week's time you ... in Paris for a year.".
- a) are living
- b) have lived
- c) will have been living

1080. Choose the right answer: "Are you leaving? Yes, but I wish I ... to go.".
    a) didn't have
    b) will not have
    c) don't have

1081. Choose the right answer: "When you are riding a bicycle you should ... the handlebars firmly.".
    a) hold
    b) hand
    c) have

1082. Choose the right answer: "If we are thinking of having a day in the country, I should listen to the weather ...".
    a) spell
    b) recording
    c) forecast

1083. Choose the right answer: "I bought a single ticket only on the bus, but my cousin bought a ... one.".
    a) new
    b) return
    c) second

1084. Choose the right answer: "How much would you ... for repairing my laptop?".
    a) cost
    b) charge
    c) pay

1085. Choose the right answer: "They ... their examinations at the end of the next month.".
    a) are going to take
    b) take
    c) took

1086. Choose the right answer: "It took years of research, but ... they found a solution.".
    a) at the end

b) in the end
c) last

1087. Choose the right answer: "Next month, my husband and I will ... for ten years.".
a) have been married
b) merry
c) have married

1088. Choose the right answer: "Tim had his big sister ... his shoes for him.".
a) tying
b) to tie
c) tie

1089. Choose the right answer: "Steven came to work at the University twenty years ... today.".
a) since
b) before
c) ago

1090. Choose the right answer: "One can become frustrated by a legal system when judges ...".
a) appear uninterested
b) fall asleep
c) are impartial

1091. Choose the right answer: "Don't worry about the last train home, as we can easily ... you up for the night.".
a) take
b) put
c) keep

1092. Choose the right answer: "The whole story is made up. It's nothing but a ... of lies.".
a) good
b) teeth
c) tissue

1093. Choose the right answer: "She is expert … drafting the minutes of a meeting.".
- a) for
- b) in
- c) with

1094. Choose the right answer: "Golf is a subject I know very … of.".
- a) few
- b) a few
- c) little

1095. Choose the right answer: "Her landlord gave her two month's … to quit.".
- a) notice
- b) warn
- c) allowance

1096. Choose the right answer: "The weather was … that we didn't go out.".
- a) too bad
- b) so bad
- c) very bad

1097. Choose the right answer: "Our plane will arrive … Hong Kong at noon.".
- a) in
- b) to
- c) at

1098. Choose the right answer: "His office is only … away.".
- a) a stone throw
- b) stone's throw
- c) stone throw

1099. Choose the right answer: "… in ill-fitting clothes, she smiled a warm welcome.".
- a) Dressed
- b) Dress
- c) Being dressed

1100. Choose the right answer: "He detested the play, for the review was not merely ..., it was ...".
    a) critical/scathing
    b) sincere/long
    c) appreciative/stinging

Set XII

1101. Choose the right answer: "There are a lot of ... beaches on these islands.".
    a) alone
    b) left
    c) deserted

1102. Choose the right answer: "I do wish ... get round to seeing a medical doctor.".
    a) you will
    b) you would
    c) you are going to

1103. Choose the right answer: "I had to go to the bank to ... some money for my holiday.".
    a) draw in
    b) pay back
    c) draw out

1104. Choose the right answer: "When I came back from holiday my suitcases were ... by the Customs Officers.".
    a) examined
    b) tested
    c) guarded

1105. Choose the right answer: "... you get to the crossroads, you will have to stop and ask for directions again.".
    a) When
    b) There
    c) While

1106. Choose the right answer: "Your boyfriend is rude! If I were you , I wouldn't stand ... it.".
    a) for
    b) by
    c) at

1107. Choose the right answer: "My sister had her camera ... from her car.".

a) robbed
b) stolen
c) lost

1108. Choose the right answer: "The two sisters don't get ... with each other very well.".
a) over
b) by
c) on

1109. Choose the right answer: "Her father began to lose his ... when he was in his seventies.".
a) view
b) look
c) sight

1110. Choose the right answer: "Her voice was so ... that I could hardly hear her.".
a) faint
b) dull
c) unnoticeable

1111. Choose the right answer: "I'll see ... the cooking tonight.".
a) at
b) to
c) for

1112. Choose the right answer: "At what time will you call ... me?".
a) for
b) at
c) to

1113. Choose the right answer: "I can assure you ... my support.".
a) from
b) at
c) of

1114. Choose the right answer: "She wanted to borrow the record from me but she was shy ... asking.".
a) with

b) of

c) to

1115. Choose the right answer: "Brian is a mechanic and his wife works …".

a) domestic

b) domestical

c) as a domestic

1116. Choose the right answer: "I really didn't want us to move there, but I was a child, I had …".

a) no say in the matter

b) no say in matter

c) no say about the matter

1117. Choose the right answer: "If I had been to that meeting, I … about it.".

a) had spoken

b) would have spoken

c) will speak

1118. Choose the right answer: "Come to see me at six o'clock. I … ready with my work by that time.".

a) have been

b) had been

c) should have been

1119. Choose the right answer: "As pretty as … = Very pretty.".

a) a fair haired girl

b) a picture

c) a swan

1120. Choose the right answer: "I was … out of 120 applicants for the position.".

a) short-listed

b) short-changed

c) short-handed

1121. Choose the right answer: "Her … is getting worse and worse. Sarah seems too afraid to speak to anyone.".

a) happiness
b) shyness
c) tiredness

1122. Choose the right answer: "The medical doctor gave the patient ... examination.".
a) a hole
b) a thorough
c) an abstract

1123. Choose the right answer: "That dress looks lovely: blue really ... you!".
a) suits
b) fits
c) pleases

1124. Choose the right answer: "I ... the bell several times but there was nobody at home.".
a) knocked
b) pulled
c) pressed

1125. Choose the right answer: "If you eat a lot of chocolate, your teeth will begin to ...".
a) decay
b) drop
c) fall

1126. Choose the right answer: "I'm afraid that it won't be possible ...".
a) for my coming
b) for me to come
c) that I come

1127. Choose the right answer: "The campers put their tent ... in a field.".
a) in
b) out
c) up

1128. Choose the right answer: "I disagree ... you about that laptop.".
a) with

b) for
c) from

1129. Choose the right answer: "We were so busy we had to ... going on holiday for two months.".
a) put off
b) put down
c) put in

1130. Choose the right answer: "They ... understand the professor, as he spoke too fast.".
a) wouldn't
b) couldn't
c) shouldn't

1131. Choose the right answer: "I don't think she could ever give ... smoking.".
a) away
b) out
c) up

1132. Choose the right answer: "... scientists have observed increased pollution in the water supply.".
a) Lately
b) Latter
c) Late

1133. Choose the right answer: "Do you approve ... hunting?".
a) on
b) of
c) in

1134. Choose the right answer: "Marry preferred to wait ... you.".
a) at
b) on
c) for

1135. Choose the right answer: "I refuse to comment ... his work.".
a) on

b) about
c) in

1136. Choose the right answer: "Their walking-tour through the amusement park never came …".
    a) off
    b) round
    c) out

1137. Choose the right answer: "I … for that job before I passed my final exams at the university.".
    a) applied
    b) had applied
    c) have applied

1138. Choose the right answer: "The boy hoped to … one of these subjects at university.".
    a) abandon
    b) discover around
    c) specialize in

1139. Choose the right answer: "I'm angry with Mary. Next time I see her, I'll give her an …".
    a) earful
    b) rip
    c) bend

1140. Choose the right answer: "Many years ago, in a strange land there lived … wise old man.".
    a) some
    b) a
    c) the

1141. Choose the right answer: "Have I … you about our new graphic card?".
    a) explained
    b) said
    c) told

1142. Choose the right answer: "This movie is by ... the best I have ever seen.".
   a) long
   b) much
   c) far

1143. Choose the right answer: "Elderly people have to live on the money they ... when they were working.".
   a) set up
   b) put aside
   c) laid up

1144. Choose the right answer: "You shouldn't call your superior ... his first name.".
   a) by
   b) in
   c) under

1145. Choose the right answer: "I've had replies to our invitations from everyone ... from Sharon.".
   a) apart
   b) only
   c) without

1146. Choose the right answer: "I had to get up early, ... I'd have missed the bus.".
   a) if not
   b) so that
   c) otherwise

1147. Choose the right answer: "I ... you to drive carefully today. The roads are icy.".
   a) recommend
   b) refer
   c) regard

1148. Choose the right answer: "I wanted to go home but my girlfriend ... on going to a park.".
   a) intended

b) insisted
c) persisted

1149. Choose the right answer: "The house ... beside the lake.".
a) rested
b) sat
c) stood

1150. Choose the right answer: "After the revolution, people ... revenge on the secret police.".
a) took
b) made
c) had

1151. Choose the right answer: "Much stricter ... must now be taken at airports.".
a) precautions
b) alarms
c) warnings

1152. Choose the right answer: "She dances really ..., doesn't she?".
a) beautiful
b) beautifully
c) beauty

1153. Choose the right answer: "The decision is yours, but I'd prefer you not ... home until next year.".
a) to leaving
b) leaving
c) to leave

1154. Choose the right answer: "The accident was terrible because there was no medical doctor ... to help.".
a) on hand
b) out of hand
c) by hand

1155. Choose the right answer: "... is known about the side-effects of the new cancer drug.".
a) All but nothing

b) Next to nothing
c) Next to anything

1156. Choose the right answer: "If I got her letter, I ... her address.".
a) know
b) would know
c) will know

1157. Choose the right answer: "We had a row but we've ... it up now.".
a) made
b) sorted
c) turned

1158. Choose the right answer: "It was ... that he happened to walk in just as we were discussing him.".
a) wretched
b) contemptible
c) unfortunate

1159. Choose the right answer: "In ... of rage he tried to kill his own sister.".
a) fit
b) period
c) mood

1160. Choose the right answer: "He was in his late sixties, with staring eyes and a ... hairline.".
a) receding
b) curly
c) bushy

1161. Choose the right answer: "The estate agent spent a ... deal of time trying to persuade her to buy the flat.".
a) great
b) large
c) big

1162. Choose the right answer: "In the pub she found herself sitting ... a well-known personality.".
a) from

b) about
c) opposite

1163. Choose the right answer: "He has always wanted to see his name in ...".
a) news
b) paper
c) print

1164. Choose the right answer: "If you ... to Boston tomorrow, telephone me first.".
a) will go
b) are going
c) had been going

1165. Choose the right answer: "There is no ... in going to university if you're not willing to learn.".
a) aim
b) point
c) purpose

1166. Choose the right answer: "The expert ... the painting carefully and said it was not authentic.".
a) watched
b) investigated
c) examined

1167. Choose the right answer: "Could you hang ... a minute? I'll be right back!".
a) on
b) in
c) on to

1168. Choose the right answer: "I've ... my wallet at home.".
a) missed
b) let
c) left

1169. Choose the right answer: "Books may be ... from the library for up to four weeks.".

a) asked
b) borrowed
c) given

1170. Choose the right answer: "She ... her parents to let her go to Spain.".
a) persuaded
b) made
c) reasoned

1171. Choose the right answer: "That's a nice coat and the colour ... you well.".
a) matched
b) suits
c) fits

1172. Choose the right answer: "... his flu, he got up and went to work.".
a) In spite
b) Even though
c) Despite

1173. Choose the right answer: "You are quite today. What have you got on your ...?".
a) mind
b) spirit
c) mood

1174. Choose the right answer: "In some countries, there is a terrible ... of food.".
a) shortness
b) shortage
c) offer

1175. Choose the right answer: "There is a beautiful ... of the old city from the terrace.".
a) view
b) vision
c) aspect

1176. Choose the right answer: "I don't like to ask people for help, but I wonder if you could ... me a favour.".

a) make
b) find
c) do

1177. Choose the right answer: "You shouldn't get so angry ... him.".
a) for
b) with
c) to

1178. Choose the right answer: "Here you are! I ... for you since three o'clock.".
a) was looking
b) am looking
c) have been looking

1179. Choose the right answer: "She has recently ... golf to provide herself with some relaxation.".
a) taken up
b) taken with
c) taken over

1180. Choose the right answer: "After several hours on the road they became ... to the fact that they would never reach the camp.".
a) dejected
b) resigned
c) disillusioned

1181. Choose the right answer: "I'm afraid I can't come to dinner on Friday. Could we put it ... until next week?".
a) off
b) away
c) up

1182. Choose the right answer: "When I visited the zoo it was crowded but on a weekday it's practically ...".
a) full
b) clear
c) empty

1183. Choose the right answer: "The ... of blood always makes him feel sick.".
    a) view
    b) sight
    c) form

1184. Choose the right answer: "They broke ... a few months ago and are now living apart.".
    a) away
    b) up
    c) into

1185. Choose the right answer: "What he says ... true but I very much doubt it.".
    a) may be
    b) will be
    c) shall be

1186. Choose the right answer: "You ... try to make your applications a bit neater.".
    a) will
    b) shall
    c) should

1187. Choose the right answer: "His shoes were so old that his ... were sticking out.".
    a) toes
    b) tips
    c) thumbs

1188. Choose the right answer: "The child was made ... everything on her plate.".
    a) ate
    b) eating
    c) to eat

1189. Choose the right answer: "You really ... have come to the party.".
    a) should
    b) can
    c) will

1190. Choose the right answer: "We didn't sign the contract because there were a number of points we couldn't agree …".
    a) in
    b) on
    c) at

1191. Choose the right answer: "You had better keep a lighter … in case you need it.".
    a) by hand
    b) in the way
    c) handy

1192. Choose the right answer: "I was shocked … her refusal.".
    a) at
    b) for
    c) with

1193. Choose the right answer: "It is rude to stare … people.".
    a) on
    b) at
    c) into

1194. Choose the right answer: "Just guess … the price of this telephone.".
    a) to
    b) from
    c) at

1195. Choose the right answer: "How can you agree with this idea when you are ignorant … the basic facts?".
    a) of
    b) in
    c) to

1196. Choose the right answer: "I'm surprised … you!".
    a) to
    b) on
    c) at

1197. Choose the right answer: "Her lesson is going to be … Monday.".
    a) in

b) on

c) at

1198. Choose the right answer: "This hotel has ... and you'll have to try your luck at others.".

a) no space

b) not rooms

c) no rooms

1199. Choose the right answer: "If I had seen this film on TV, I ... to the cinema to see it.".

a) wouldn't have gone

b) didn't go

c) wouldn't go

1200. Choose the right answer: "What ... for the last three weeks?".

a) are you doing

b) have you been doing

c) did you do

Set XIII

1201. Choose the right answer: "A vacuum will neither conduct heat nor …".
   a) the transmission of sound waves
   b) sound waves are transmitted
   c) transmit sound waves

1202. Choose the right answer: "This man is … of modern fiction.".
   a) the molders one
   b) one of the molders
   c) who is one of the molders

1203. Choose the right answer: "Your new car … as well as speedy.".
   a) looks comfortable
   b) comfortably looks
   c) looks is comfortable

1204. Choose the right answer: "A problem in the construction of new buildings …".
   a) is because windows are eliminated but air conditioners don't work good
   b) is they have eliminating windows and still don't have good air conditioning
   c) is that windows have been eliminated while air conditioning systems have not been improved

1205. Choose the right answer: "… received law degrees as today.".
   a) Women who have never
   b) Never have so many women
   c) The women aren't ever

1206. Choose the right answer: "Some embarrassing situations occur … a misunderstanding.".
   a) because of
   b) for
   c) of

1207. Choose the right answer: "Put plants … a window so that they will get enough light.".

a) next to
b) nearly
c) near of

1208. Choose the right answer: "A computer is usually chosen because of its simplicity of operation ... its capacity to store information.".
a) the same
b) as well as
c) as well

1209. Choose the right answer: "... is no way to tell the exact number of heroin addicts.".
a) What
b) Each
c) There

1210. Choose the right answer: "Today's keyboard is nearly ... Sholes keyboard.".
a) the same as
b) as same as
c) a same one as

1211. Choose the right answer: "Spectrographs ... possible to analyze the human voice.".
a) makes it
b) are made
c) make it

1212. Choose the right answer: "The seed heads of teasel plants raise the nap on coarse tweed cloth ... than do the machine tools.".
a) more efficiently
b) more efficient
c) most efficient

1213. Choose the right answer: "It is generally believed that an MBA degree is good for a career in ...".
a) one business
b) business
c) a business

1214. Choose the right answer: "Zoo animals must have a dentist ... their teeth.".
    a) filled
    b) to be filled
    c) fill

1215. Choose the right answer: "He ... in order to prove his theories of cultural diffusion.".
    a) sailing specifically charted courses
    b) has sailed specifically charted courses
    c) they sail specifically charted courses

1216. Choose the right answer: "Psychologists believe that incentives ... to increase our productivity.".
    a) make us want
    b) making us want
    c) makes us wanting

1217. Choose the right answer: "The blue whale is ... known animal.".
    a) the large
    b) most largest
    c) the largest

1218. Choose the right answer: "Strauss finished ... two of his compositions before his tenth birthday.".
    a) writing
    b) to write
    c) written

1219. Choose the right answer: "A dividend is ... the only benefit for a shareholder.".
    a) nor
    b) none
    c) not

1220. Choose the right answer: "Deserts produce less than 1 gram of plant growth ... from every square yard.".
    a) the day
    b) one day
    c) some day

1221. Choose the right answer: "The artistic medium of clay is ... that images have been found near the remains of fires from the Ice Age.".
	a) so old
	b) oldest
	c) old

1222. Choose the right answer: "So far there is no vaccine ... in sight for the common cold.".
	a) or curing
	b) has cured
	c) or cure

1223. Choose the right answer: "Children just love computer games, ... many adults.".
	a) not
	b) as do
	c) so

1224. Choose the right answer: "She wanted to serve some coffee to her guests; however, ...".
	a) she hadn't many sugar
	b) she did not have much sugar
	c) there was not a great amount of sugars

1225. Choose the right answer: "When friends insist on ... expensive gifts, it makes most people uncomfortable.".
	a) them to accept
	b) they accept
	c) their accepting

1226. Choose the right answer: "Most students don't like local coffee and ...".
	a) neither do I
	b) I don't too
	c) neither don't I

1227. Choose the right answer: "Burrowing animals provide paths for water in soil and so do the roots of plants ...".
	a) decaying and they dying

        b) when they die and decay
        c) when they will die and decaying

1228. Choose the right answer: "Bees ... display distinct preferences for different colors, but are also sensitive to ultraviolet light.".
        a) not only
        b) can only
        c) only

1229. Choose the right answer: "The birth of a girl is welcomed with an enthusiasm ... to that of a boy.".
        a) they are equal
        b) equally
        c) equal

1230. Choose the right answer: "Some adopted people who have found who their natural parents are wish that they ... the experience of meeting.".
        a) hadn't had
        b) didn't have had
        c) hadn't

1231. Choose the right answer: "... through a telescope, this planet appears to go through changes in size.".
        a) Seeing
        b) When seen
        c) It has seen

1232. Choose the right answer: "Ice should be applied immediately when an athlete suffers an injury to ... leg.".
        a) his
        b) the
        c) an

1233. Choose the right answer: "Unless protected area are established, many animals face ... of extinction.".
        a) possibly
        b) to be possible
        c) the possibility

1234. Choose the right answer: "A communications satellite orbits the earth at the same rate that the earth revolves ... over a fixed point on the surface.".
    a) so can remain
    b) it can remain
    c) so that it can remain

1235. Choose the right answer: "... is not a new idea.".
    a) The planning of cities
    b) Plan cities
    c) To planning cities

1236. Choose the right answer: "Many architects insist on ... eco-friendly materials.".
    a) use
    b) using
    c) to use

1237. Choose the right answer: "... were first viewed through a telescope by Galileo.".
    a) Jupiter's moons
    b) Jupiter has moons
    c) Surrounded by moons, Jupiter

1238. Choose the right answer: "Photography changed dramatically ... introduced paper-based film.".
    a) when it was
    b) when was
    c) when Eastman

1239. Choose the right answer: "Before ... he took part in a series of debates.".
    a) the Civil War with
    b) the Civil War
    c) it happened that the Civil War

1240. Choose the right answer: "The rabbit scurried away in fright ...".
    a) when it heard movement in the bushes
    b) after it was hearing moving inside of the bushes
    c) the movement among the bushes having been hear

1241. Choose the right answer: "... thirteen states in the original United States.".
    a) There were
    b) So were
    c) Were

1242. Choose the right answer: "Tuna, ..., may weigh up to 900 pounds.".
    a) is the sea giant
    b) the sea of the giant
    c) one of the sea giants

1243. Choose the right answer: "... there is a close correlation between stress and illness.".
    a) Believed some psychologists
    b) Some psychologists believe
    c) Some psychologists believing

1244. Choose the right answer: "... is used in soups.".
    a) An herb is inexpensive parsley,
    b) Inexpensive parsley, herb
    c) Parsley, an inexpensive herb,

1245. Choose the right answer: "..., common weedy plants, are popular among children.".
    a) Dandelions
    b) Known as dandelions
    c) Which are dandelions

1246. Choose the right answer: "One of the professor's greatest attributes is ...".
    a) when he gives lectures
    b) his ability to lecture
    c) how in the manner that he lectures

1247. Choose the right answer: "... two major championships on the professional golf tour.".
    a) In all
    b) There are
    c) They are

1248. Choose the right answer: "Some farmers use several methods to prevent top soil …".
     a) to run off
     b) to running off
     c) from running off

1249. Choose the right answer: "The country's first globe maker was Mr. Smith, who … and blacksmith in his earlier life.".
     a) had been a farmer
     b) farming
     c) being a farmer

1250. Choose the right answer: "He … the 1968 Nobel Prize for medicine.".
     a) to award
     b) awarding
     c) was awarded

1251. Choose the right answer: "… Social Security Acts were written to insure workers against unemployment.".
     a) The
     b) For the
     c) What the

1252. Choose the right answer: "The more Sarah worked …".
     a) she achieved not enough
     b) she was achieving less
     c) the less she achieved

1253. Choose the right answer: "Having been selected to represent our association, …".
     a) a speech had to be given by he
     b) he gave a short acceptance speech
     c) the members congratulated him speech

1254. Choose the right answer: "The decomposition of animals at the bottom of the sea results in an accumulation of … in porous rocks.".
     a) an oil
     b) oil
     c) some oiling

1255. Choose the right answer: "A perennial is ... for more than two years.".
    a) any plant continuing growth
    b) any plant it continuing to grow
    c) any plant that continues to grow

1256. Choose the right answer: "Hybrids have one more ... per plant than other varieties.".
    a) ear of corn
    b) corn's earing
    c) corn ears

1257. Choose the right answer: "Some members are insisting that changes in the social security system ... made.".
    a) being
    b) will
    c) be

1258. Choose the right answer: "The javelin used in competition must be between 260 and 270 centimeters ...".
    a) it is long
    b) in length
    c) whose length

1259. Choose the right answer: "The closer to one of the earth's poles, the greater ... gravitational force.".
    a) it has
    b) the
    c) is

1260. Choose the right answer: "Pigs ... some DNA characteristics with human beings.".
    a) sharing
    b) are shared
    c) share

1261. Choose the right answer: "Fire-resistant material are used to retard ... of modern aircraft.".
    a) damage to the passenger cabin

b) a damage to the passenger cabin
c) passenger cabin's damages

1262. Choose the right answer: "Because our country doesn't have much oil anymore, imported oil ... used more and more.".
a) will
b) is being
c) must

1263. Choose the right answer: "The FDA was set up ... that maintain standards for the sale of food and drugs.".
a) enforcing laws
b) enforced the laws
c) to enforce the laws

1264. Choose the right answer: "If a ruby is heated it ... temporarily lose its color.".
a) will
b) has
c) does

1265. Choose the right answer: "Robots are being used increasingly in industry as they can work faster and ...".
a) don't as easily tire
b) don't too easily tire
c) don't tire easily

1266. Choose the right answer: "The algebra of sets ... Boolean algebra.".
a) is called
b) called
c) known as

1267. Choose the right answer: "That magnificent ... temple was constructed by the Japanese.".
a) nine-century-old
b) old-nine-centuries
c) nine-centuries-old

1268. Choose the right answer: "... the formation of the Sun began with the condensation of an interstellar cloud.".

a) Accepted that
b) It is accepted that
c) That is accepted

1269. Choose the right answer: "… in Shanghai than in any other city in China.".
a) More people live
b) Most people live
c) It has most people live

1270. Choose the right answer: "That most natural time units are not simple multiples of each other … in constructing a calendar.".
a) a primary problem
b) a primary problem is
c) is a primary problem

1271. Choose the right answer: "In this country more than 50 percent of all high school students who … continue their education.".
a) will
b) graduate
c) can

1272. Choose the right answer: "Although this area is densely populated, … live in the northern part of the state.".
a) few people
b) a little people
c) a little of people

1273. Choose the right answer: "Waiters who serve … deserve at least a 15 percent tip.".
a) in a courteous manner
b) with courtesy in their manner
c) courteously

1274. Choose the right answer: "If water is heated to 100 degrees C … as steam.".
a) it will boil and escape
b) it is boiling and escaping
c) it would boil and escape

1275. Choose the right answer: "The total production of corn is ... all other cereal crops combined.".
    a) more than that of
    b) more of
    c) more that

1276. Choose the right answer: "By the time a baby has reached his first birthday, he should ... sit up.".
    a) able to
    b) be able to
    c) to be able

1277. Choose the right answer: "The sport of hang gliding ... by the FAA.".
    a) regulated it
    b) that it was regulated
    c) is regulated

1278. Choose the right answer: "It is recommended ... all children be vaccinated against a variety of diseases.".
    a) that
    b) for
    c) when

1279. Choose the right answer: "This settlement ... in 1702.".
    a) founded
    b) colonists arrived
    c) was established

1280. Choose the right answer: "... of the play introduces the cast of characters.".
    a) The act first
    b) Act one
    c) Act first

1281. Choose the right answer: "... owe much of their success as a group to their powers of migration.".
    a) Birds
    b) A bird
    c) That birds

1282. Choose the right answer: "Even if the unemployment rate ... sharply, the drop may still be temporary.".
 a) to drop
 b) dropping
 c) drops

1283. Choose the right answer: "She was very angry that her mail from home ...".
 a) opened
 b) had been opened
 c) was opening

1284. Choose the right answer: "His wife ... told that he had had an aviation accident.".
 a) was
 b) is
 c) had to

1285. Choose the right answer: "The woman read an advertisement ... the newspaper about a house to rent.".
 a) out of
 b) from
 c) in

1286. Choose the right answer: "They went to the store to buy knives, spoons and ...".
 a) eating tools
 b) silverwear
 c) glasses

1287. Choose the right answer: "Some of the current international problems we are now facing ...".
 a) are the result of misunderstandings
 b) linguistic incompetence
 c) are because of not understanding themselves

1288. Choose the right answer: "The crime rate has continued to rise despite efforts to curb ...".
 a) them

b) it
c) its

1289. Choose the right answer: "... of commodities by air began in the 1930s.".
   a) A ship
   b) To ship
   c) The shipping

1290. Choose the right answer: "Ten national sites are known as parks, twenty as monuments and ...".
   a) the other one hundred as historical sites
   b) the another one hundred as historic site
   c) one hundred more as historical site

1291. Choose the right answer: "... daily promotes physical well-being.".
   a) Having exercised
   b) Exercising
   c) For exercising

1292. Choose the right answer: "Scientific community had hoped that the field of transplantation ..., the shortage of organ donors has curtailed research.".
   a) progressing
   b) would progress
   c) had progressed

1293. Choose the right answer: "... apples are grown in this region.".
   a) The best
   b) The most good
   c) The better

1294. Choose the right answer: "Countries may ... the World Bank for development.".
   a) lend large sums of money from
   b) lend large sums of money
   c) borrow large sums of money from

1295. Choose the right answer: "Mount Everest ... to more than twenty-nine thousand feet.".

a) arises
b) rises
c) raises

1296. Choose the right answer: "... migrate long distances is well documented.".
a) That birds
b) Birds that
c) It is that birds

1297. Choose the right answer: "To relieve pressure in the skull, ... into the blood.".
a) you will inject a strong solution
b) a strong solution of glucose will inject purely
c) inject a strong solution of pure glucose

1298. Choose the right answer: "A slipped disk is a condition ... the intervertebral disk protrudes.".
a) that
b) in which
c) what

1299. Choose the right answer: "The pirate offered his services to the government, ... and received a full pardon.".
a) fought in the battle
b) the battle was fought
c) fighting the battle

1300. Choose the right answer: "The facilities of the older hospital ...".
a) is as good or better than the new hospital
b) are as good as or better than the new hospital
c) are as good as or better than those of the new hospital

Answers

1.b	2.a	3.c	4.b	5.c	6.a	7.b	8.c	9.a	10.b
11.a	12.c	13.b	14.a	15.b	16.c	17.a	18.c	19.a	20.b
21.a	22.c	23.b	24.a	25.c	26.a	27.b	28.b	29.a	30.c
31.c	32.a	33.b	34.b	35.c	36.b	37.a	38.b	39.c	40.a
41.a	42.c	43.c	44.a	45.b	46.a	47.b	48.b	49.c	50.b
51.a	52.c	53.b	54.c	55.a	56.b	57.c	58.b	59.b	60.a
61.c	62.b	63.b	64.a	65.c	66.b	67.a	68.c	69.b	70.a
71.c	72.c	73.a	74.b	75.b	76.b	77.c	78.a	79.b	80.c
81.c	82.a	83.b	84.b	85.a	86.c	87.a	88.b	89.b	90.c
91.c	92.a	93.b	94.c	95.c	96.a	97.b	98.a	99.b	100.c

101.a	102.c	103.b	104.c	105.a	106.b	107.c	108.a	109.c
110.b	111.b	112.a	113.c	114.a	115.b	116.b	117.c	118.a
119.c	120.c	121.b	122.a	123.c	124.b	125.a	126.b	127.c
128.c	129.b	130.a	131.b	132.c	133.a	134.b	135.c	136.a
137.b	138.c	139.a	140.b	141.b	142.c	143.a	144.c	145.b
146.b	147.a	148.c	149.a	150.c	151.a	152.b	153.b	154.c
155.a	156.c	157.b	158.b	159.a	160.c	161.a	162.b	163.c
164.a	165.b	166.c	167.a	168.b	169.c	170.a	171.b	172.c
173.a	174.b	175.c	176.a	177.c	178.b	179.a	180.c	181.a
182.b	183.c	184.b	185.a	186.a	187.b	188.c	189.a	190.b
191.b	192.c	193.a	194.a	195.b	196.c	197.a	198.b	199.c
200.a	201.c	202.a	203.b	204.c	205.a	206.c	207.b	208.b
209.a	210.c	211.b	212.c	213.a	214.a	215.b	216.c	217.a
218.b	219.b	220.a	221.c	222.c	223.a	224.b	225.a	226.c
227.c	228.b	229.a	230.c	231.a	232.b	233.b	234.c	235.a
236.b	237.c	238.a	239.b	240.a	241.c	242.a	243.b	244.c
245.b	246.c	247.a	248.a	249.c	250.c	251.a	252.b	253.c
254.b	255.a	256.b	257.c	258.a	259.b	260.c	261.b	262.c
263.a	264.b	265.a	266.b	267.c	268.a	269.b	270.c	271.a
272.b	273.a	274.c	275.b	276.c	277.c	278.a	279.b	280.c
281.b	282.a	283.c	284.a	285.c	286.c	287.b	288.a	289.c
290.c	291.a	292.b	293.a	294.c	295.b	296.a	297.c	298.b
299.c	300.a	301.b	302.c	303.b	304.a	305.a	306.b	307.c
308.b	309.b	310.a	311.c	312.b	313.a	314.b	315.c	316.a
317.c	318.c	319.b	320.a	321.a	322.c	323.b	324.b	325.c
326.a	327.c	328.b	329.a	330.c	331.a	332.c	333.c	334.a
335.c	336.a	337.b	338.a	339.c	340.b	341.b	342.a	343.b
344.c	345.b	346.a	347.b	348.b	349.c	350.a	351.b	352.c
353.a	354.b	355.c	356.b	357.b	358.c	359.a	360.b	361.b
362.a	363.c	364.b	365.c	366.a	367.b	368.c	369.a	370.b
371.c	372.a	373.b	374.c	375.b	376.a	377.c	378.a	379.b
380.c	381.b	382.a	383.c	384.b	385.a	386.c	387.b	388.b
389.c	390.a	391.a	392.c	393.b	394.a	395.b	396.c	397.a
398.c	399.b	400.a	401.b	402.c	403.a	404.b	405.b	406.c
407.a	408.c	409.b	410.b	411.c	412.a	413.b	414.c	415.a

416.b	417.a	418.b	419.c	420.a	421.b	422.c	423.b	424.a
425.c	426.b	427.a	428.c	429.a	430.b	431.c	432.b	433.a

434.c	435.b	436.a	437.c	438.b	439.a	440.b	441.a	442.c
443.c	444.a	445.b	446.c	447.a	448.b	449.b	450.c	451.b
452.a	453.c	454.b	455.a	456.b	457.c	458.a	459.b	460.a
461.c	462.a	463.b	464.a	465.c	466.b	467.b	468.a	469.c
470.b	471.c	472.a	473.b	474.b	475.a	476.c	477.a	478.b
479.a	480.c	481.a	482.b	483.a	484.a	485.b	486.a	487.b
488.c	489.a	490.b	491.c	492.a	493.c	494.b	495.a	496.b
497.b	498.c	499.a	500.a	501.b	502.c	503.a	504.c	505.b
506.a	507.b	508.c	509.b	510.a	511.a	512.c	513.b	514.a
515.b	516.c	517.a	518.c	519.b	520.a	521.b	522.a	523.c
524.a	525.b	526.b	527.c	528.a	529.c	530.a	531.b	532.c
533.a	534.b	535.c	536.a	537.b	538.c	539.b	540.a	541.b
542.c	543.b	544.a	545.a	546.c	547.b	548.b	549.a	550.c
551.b	552.a	553.c	554.a	555.c	556.a	557.b	558.c	559.b
560.a	561.a	562.c	563.a	564.b	565.b	566.c	567.a	568.c
569.b	570.a	571.c	572.a	573.c	574.b	575.a	576.c	577.b
578.a	579.a	580.c	581.a	582.b	583.c	584.b	585.c	586.a
587.b	588.c	589.a	590.a	591.c	592.a	593.b	594.c	595.a
596.b	597.c	598.a	599.b	600.c	601.b	602.a	603.c	604.c
605.a	606.b	607.b	608.c	609.a	610.b	611.a	612.c	613.c
614.b	615.a	616.b	617.c	618.a	619.c	620.b	621.c	622.a
623.b	624.b	625.a	626.c	627.b	628.a	629.b	630.c	631.b
632.b	633.a	634.c	635.b	636.b	637.a	638.b	639.c	640.a
641.c	642.b	643.a	644.b	645.c	646.a	647.c	648.a	649.b
650.b	651.a	652.b	653.c	654.a	655.c	656.b	657.a	658.c
659.a	660.b	661.a	662.c	663.b	664.a	665.c	666.b	667.b
668.a	669.a	670.c	671.c	672.a	673.b	674.b	675.a	676.c
677.a	678.b	679.c	680.a	681.b	682.a	683.c	684.c	685.b
686.a	687.b	688.b	689.b	690.a	691.c	692.a	693.b	694.a
695.c	696.a	697.b	698.c	699.a	700.b	701.c	702.a	703.b
704.b	705.c	706.a	707.c	708.b	709.a	710.c	711.a	712.c
713.b	714.a	715.c	716.a	717.b	718.c	719.a	720.b	721.b
722.c	723.a	724.b	725.a	726.c	727.a	728.b	729.c	730.a
731.b	732.a	733.c	734.a	735.b	736.c	737.b	738.a	739.c
740.a	741.c	742.a	743.b	744.c	745.c	746.b	747.c	748.a
749.a	750.c	751.b	752.b	753.a	754.c	755.b	756.b	757.a
758.c	759.b	760.a	761.b	762.c	763.a	764.b	765.c	766.a
767.a	768.c	769.b	770.a	771.b	772.a	773.c	774.a	775.b
776.c	777.a	778.b	779.b	780.a	781.c	782.a	783.b	784.b
785.a	786.b	787.c	788.c	789.a	790.b	791.c	792.a	793.b

794.c	795.a	796.b	797.c	798.a	799.b	800.c	801.a	802.b
803.c	804.a	805.b	806.a	807.a	808.a	809.c	810.b	811.a
812.b	813.c	814.a	815.b	816.c	817.b	818.a	819.b	820.c
821.b	822.a	823.c	824.c	825.a	826.b	827.c	828.a	829.c
830.a	831.a	832.b	833.c	834.b	835.a	836.c	837.b	838.a
839.c	840.b	841.b	842.a	843.c	844.b	845.a	846.c	847.b
848.c	849.a	850.a	851.b	852.b	853.b	854.a	855.c	856.a
857.b	858.c	859.a	860.b	861.a	862.c	863.b	864.b	865.a
866.c	867.c	868.a	869.b	870.a	871.c	872.b	873.c	874.a
875.b	876.c	877.a	878.b	879.a	880.c	881.b	882.a	883.c
884.a	885.b	886.c	887.c	888.a	889.b	890.c	891.a	892.c

893.b	894.a	895.c	896.c	897.a	898.b	899.c	900.a	901.b
902.b	903.c	904.a	905.b	906.a	907.c	908.b	909.a	910.b
911.c	912.b	913.b	914.a	915.a	916.c	917.c	918.a	919.b
920.a	921.b	922.c	923.a	924.c	925.b	926.a	927.c	928.a
929.b	930.c	931.b	932.b	933.c	934.a	935.a	936.b	937.a
938.c	939.b	940.a	941.c	942.c	943.b	944.c	945.a	946.b
947.a	948.b	949.c	950.a	951.b	952.c	953.a	954.b	955.a
956.c	957.b	958.a	959.b	960.c	961.a	962.b	963.a	964.a
965.c	966.b	967.a	968.a	969.c	970.b	971.a	972.c	973.b
974.b	975.a	976.c	977.a	978.b	979.c	980.b	981.a	982.b
983.c	984.b	985.a	986.b	987.c	988.a	989.c	990.b	991.a
992.c	993.a	994.b	995.a	996.c	997.a	998.b	999.a	1000.c
1001.a	1002.b	1003.a	1004.c	1005.b	1006.c	1007.a	1008.b	1009.b
1010.a	1011.b	1012.a	1013.c	1014.b	1015.a	1016.c	1017.b	1018.a
1019.c	1020.a	1021.a	1022.b	1023.c	1024.a	1025.b	1026.a	1027.c
1028.b	1029.a	1030.b	1031.c	1032.b	1033.a	1034.b	1035.a	1036.c
1037.c	1038.a	1039.b	1040.a	1041.c	1042.b	1043.a	1044.b	1045.c
1046.c	1047.b	1048.b	1049.a	1050.c	1051.a	1052.b	1053.c	1054.b
1055.a	1056.b	1057.c	1058.b	1059.a	1060.b	1061.b	1062.c	1063.b
1064.a	1065.b	1066.c	1067.a	1068.b	1069.c	1070.a	1071.b	1072.a
1073.c	1074.b	1075.c	1076.a	1077.b	1078.a	1079.c	1080.a	1081.a
1082.c	1083.b	1084.b	1085.a	1086.b	1087.a	1088.c	1089.c	1090.c
1091.b	1092.c	1093.b	1094.c	1095.a	1096.b	1097.c	1098.b	1099.a
1100.a	1101.c	1102.b	1103.c	1104.a	1105.a	1106.a	1107.b	1108.c
1109.c	1110.a	1111.b	1112.a	1113.c	1114.b	1115.c	1116.a	1117.b
1118.c	1119.b	1120.a	1121.b	1122.b	1123.a	1124.c	1125.a	1126.b
1127.c	1128.a	1129.a	1130.b	1131.c	1132.a	1133.b	1134.c	1135.a
1136.a	1137.b	1138.c	1139.a	1140.b	1141.c	1142.c	1143.b	1144.a
1145.a	1146.c	1147.a	1148.b	1149.c	1150.a	1151.a	1152.b	1153.c
1154.a	1155.b	1156.b	1157.a	1158.c	1159.b	1160.a	1161.a	1162.c
1163.c	1164.b	1165.b	1166.c	1167.a	1168.c	1169.b	1170.a	1171.c
1172.c	1173.a	1174.b	1175.a	1176.c	1177.b	1178.c	1179.a	1180.b
1181.a	1182.c	1183.b	1184.b	1185.a	1186.c	1187.a	1188.c	1189.a
1190.b	1191.c	1192.a	1193.b	1194.c	1195.a	1196.c	1197.b	1198.c
1199.a	1200.b	1201.c	1202.b	1203.a	1204.c	1205.b	1206.a	1207.a
1208.b	1209.c	1210.a	1211.c	1212.a	1213.b	1214.c	1215.b	1216.a
1217.c	1218.a	1219.c	1220.b	1221.a	1222.c	1223.b	1224.b	1225.c
1226.a	1227.b	1228.a	1229.c	1230.a	1231.b	1232.a	1233.c	1234.c
1235.a	1236.b	1237.a	1238.c	1239.b	1240.a	1241.a	1242.c	1243.b
1244.c	1245.a	1246.b	1247.b	1248.c	1249.a	1250.c	1251.a	1252.c
1253.b	1254.b	1255.c	1256.a	1257.c	1258.b	1259.b	1260.c	1261.a
1262.b	1263.c	1264.a	1265.c	1266.a	1267.a	1268.b	1269.a	1270.c
1271.b	1272.a	1273.c	1274.a	1275.a	1276.b	1277.c	1278.a	1279.c
1280.b	1281.a	1282.c	1283.b	1284.a	1285.c	1286.c	1287.a	1288.b
1289.c	1290.a	1291.b	1292.b	1293.a	1294.c	1295.b	1296.a	1297.c
1298.b	1299.a	1300.c						

Conclusion

In conclusion I want to thank you for buying my book and I hope you find it useful. Please pay attention to further personally crafted "TOEFL Grammar with Answer Key" books which I intend to release. This will certainly be one of the best series of grammar exercises.

Write a review

I am constantly improving my books and my work, trying to deliver to my readers the best quality information. To improve my work and myself as a human being, I need organic reviews to know where I am wrong or where I have made mistakes. Remember, there is no such thing as a perfect book, it needs updates all the time, especially if it's digital. If this book has been useful to you, please, write a review with all your thoughts. It won't take more than 1 minute. If you didn't like something from this book, please contact me and I will try to solve your problem.

Honestly,

Daniel B. Smith

Made in the USA
Middletown, DE
02 June 2025